D0074413

The Law School Admission Council (LSAC) is a nonprofit corporation that provides unique, state-of-the-art admission products and services to ease the admission process for law schools and their applicants worldwide. Currently, 220 law schools in the United States, Canada, and Australia are members of the Council and benefit from LSAC's services.

LSAC fees, policies, and procedures relating to, but not limited to, test registration, test administration, test score reporting, misconduct and irregularities, Credential Assembly Service (CAS), and other matters may change without notice at any time. Up-to-date LSAC policies and procedures are available at LSAC.org.

ISBN-13: 978-0-9907186-9-7

Print number
10 9 8 7 6 5 4 3 2 1

TABLE OF CONTENTS

The Law School Admission Test is a half-day standardized test required for admission to all ABA-approved law schools, most Canadian law schools, and many other law schools. It consists of five 35-minute sections of multiple-choice questions. Four of the five sections contribute to the test taker's score. These sections include one Reading Comprehension section, one Analytical Reasoning section, and two Logical Reasoning sections. The unscored section, commonly referred to as the variable section, typically is used to pretest new test questions or to preequate new test forms. The placement of this section in the LSAT will vary. A 35-minute writing sample is administered at the end of the test. The writing sample is not scored by LSAC, but copies are sent to all law schools to which you apply. The score scale for the LSAT is 120 to 180.

The LSAT is designed to measure skills considered essential for success in law school: the reading and comprehension of complex texts with accuracy and insight; the organization and management of information and the ability to draw reasonable inferences from it; the ability to think critically; and the analysis and evaluation of the reasoning and arguments of others.

The LSAT provides a standard measure of acquired reading and verbal reasoning skills that law schools can use as one of several factors in assessing applicants.

For up-to-date information about LSAC's services, go to our website, LSAC.org.

SCORING

Your LSAT score is based on the number of questions you answer correctly (the raw score). There is no deduction for incorrect answers, and all questions count equally. In other words, there is no penalty for guessing.

Test Score Accuracy—Reliability and Standard Error of Measurement

Candidates perform at different levels on different occasions for reasons quite unrelated to the characteristics of a test itself. The accuracy of test scores is best described by the use of two related statistical terms: reliability and standard error of measurement.

Reliability is a measure of how consistently a test measures the skills being assessed. The higher the reliability coefficient for a test, the more certain we can be that test takers would get very similar scores if they took the test again.

LSAC reports an internal consistency measure of reliability for every test form. Reliability can vary from 0.00 to 1.00, and a test with no measurement error would have a reliability coefficient of 1.00 (never attained in practice). Reliability coefficients for past LSAT forms have ranged from .90 to .95, indicating a high degree of consistency for these tests. LSAC expects the reliability of the LSAT to continue to fall within the same range.

LSAC also reports the amount of measurement error associated with each test form, a concept known as the standard error of measurement (SEM). The SEM, which is usually about 2.6 points, indicates how close a test taker's observed score is likely to be to his or her true score. True scores are theoretical scores that would be obtained from perfectly reliable tests with no measurement error—scores never known in practice.

Score bands, or ranges of scores that contain a test taker's true score a certain percentage of the time, can be derived using the SEM. LSAT score bands are constructed by adding and subtracting the (rounded) SEM to and from an actual LSAT score (e.g., the LSAT score, plus or minus 3 points). Scores near 120 or 180 have asymmetrical bands. Score bands constructed in this manner will contain an individual's true score approximately 68 percent of the time.

Measurement error also must be taken into account when comparing LSAT scores of two test takers. It is likely that small differences in scores are due to measurement error rather than to meaningful differences in ability. The standard error of score differences provides some guidance as to the importance of differences between two scores. The standard error of score differences is approximately 1.4 times larger than the standard error of measurement for the individual scores.

Thus, a test score should be regarded as a useful but approximate measure of a test taker's abilities as measured by the test, not as an exact determination of his or her abilities. LSAC encourages law schools to examine the range of scores within the interval that probably contains the test taker's true score (e.g., the test taker's score band) rather than solely interpret the reported score alone.

Adjustments for Variation in Test Difficulty

All test forms of the LSAT reported on the same score scale are designed to measure the same abilities, but one test form may be slightly easier or more difficult than another. The scores from different test forms are made comparable through a statistical procedure known as equating. As a result of equating, a given scaled score earned on different test forms reflects the same level of ability.

Research on the LSAT

Summaries of LSAT validity studies and other LSAT research can be found in member law school libraries and at LSAC.org.

To Inquire About Test Questions

If you find what you believe to be an error or ambiguity in a test question that affects your response to the question, contact LSAC by e-mail: LSATTS@LSAC.org, or write to Law School Admission Council, Test Development Group, PO Box 40, Newtown, PA 18940-0040.

HOW THIS PREPTEST DIFFERS FROM AN ACTUAL LSAT

This PrepTest is made up of the scored sections and writing sample from the actual disclosed LSAT administered in June 2015. However, it does not contain the extra, variable section that is used to pretest new test items of one of the three multiple-choice question types. The three multiple-choice question types may be in a different order in an actual LSAT than in this PrepTest. This is because the order of these question types is intentionally varied for each administration of the test.

THE THREE LSAT MULTIPLE-CHOICE QUESTION TYPES

The multiple-choice questions that make up most of the LSAT reflect a broad range of academic disciplines and are intended to give no advantage to candidates from a particular academic background.

The five sections of the test contain three different question types. The following material presents a general discussion of the nature of each question type and some strategies that can be used in answering them.

Analytical Reasoning Questions

Analytical Reasoning questions are designed to assess the ability to consider a group of facts and rules, and, given those facts and rules, determine what could or must be true. The specific scenarios associated with these questions are usually unrelated to law, since they are intended to be accessible to a wide range of test takers. However, the skills tested parallel those involved in determining what could or must be the case given a set of regulations, the terms of a contract, or the facts of a legal case in relation to the law. In Analytical Reasoning questions, you are asked to reason deductively from a set of statements and rules or principles that describe relationships among persons, things, or events.

Analytical Reasoning questions appear in sets, with each set based on a single passage. The passage used for each set of questions describes common ordering relationships or grouping relationships, or a combination of both types of relationships. Examples include scheduling employees for work shifts, assigning instructors to class sections, ordering tasks according to priority, and distributing grants for projects.

Analytical Reasoning questions test a range of deductive reasoning skills. These include:

- Comprehending the basic structure of a set of relationships by determining a complete solution to the problem posed (for example, an acceptable seating arrangement of all six diplomats around a table)

- Reasoning with conditional ("if-then") statements and recognizing logically equivalent formulations of such statements

- Inferring what could be true or must be true from given facts and rules

- Inferring what could be true or must be true from given facts and rules together with new information in the form of an additional or substitute fact or rule

- Recognizing when two statements are logically equivalent in context by identifying a condition or rule that could replace one of the original conditions while still resulting in the same possible outcomes

Analytical Reasoning questions reflect the kinds of detailed analyses of relationships and sets of constraints that a law student must perform in legal problem solving. For example, an Analytical Reasoning passage might describe six diplomats being seated around a table, following certain rules of protocol as to who can sit where. You, the test taker, must answer questions about the logical implications of given and new information. For example, you may be asked who can sit between diplomats X and Y, or who cannot sit next to X if W sits next to Y. Similarly, if you were a student in law school, you might be asked to analyze a scenario involving a set of particular circumstances and a set of governing rules in the form of constitutional provisions, statutes, administrative codes, or prior rulings that have been upheld. You might then be asked to determine the legal options in the scenario: what is required given the scenario, what is permissible given the scenario, and what is prohibited given the scenario. Or you might be asked to develop a "theory" for the case: when faced with an incomplete set of facts about the case, you must fill in the picture based on what is implied by the facts that are known. The problem could be elaborated by the addition of new information or hypotheticals.

No formal training in logic is required to answer these questions correctly. Analytical Reasoning questions are intended to be answered using knowledge, skills, and reasoning ability generally expected of college students and graduates.

Suggested Approach

Some people may prefer to answer first those questions about a passage that seem less difficult and then those that seem more difficult. In general, it is best to finish one passage before starting on another, because much time can be lost in returning to a passage and reestablishing familiarity with its relationships. However, if you are having great difficulty on one particular set of questions and are spending too much time on them, it may be to your advantage to skip that set of questions and go on to the next passage, returning to the problematic set of questions after you have finished the other questions in the section.

Do not assume that because the conditions for a set of questions look long or complicated, the questions based on those conditions will be especially difficult.

Read the passage carefully. Careful reading and analysis are necessary to determine the exact nature of the relationships involved in an Analytical Reasoning passage. Some relationships are fixed (for example, P and R must always work on the same project). Other relationships are variable (for example, Q must be assigned to either team 1 or team 3). Some relationships that are not stated explicitly in the conditions are implied by and can be deduced from those that are stated (for example, if one condition about paintings in a display specifies that Painting K must be to the left of Painting Y, and another specifies that Painting W must be to the left of Painting K, then it can be deduced that Painting W must be to the left of Painting Y).

In reading the conditions, do not introduce unwarranted assumptions. For instance, in a set of questions establishing relationships of height and weight among the members of a team, do not assume that a person who is taller than another person must weigh more than that person. As another example, suppose a set involves ordering and a question in the set asks what must be true if both X and Y must be earlier than Z; in this case, do not assume that X must be earlier than Y merely because X is mentioned before Y. All the information needed to answer each question is provided in the passage and the question itself.

The conditions are designed to be as clear as possible. Do not interpret the conditions as if they were intended to trick you. For example, if a question asks how many people could be eligible to serve on a committee, consider only those people named in the passage unless directed otherwise. When in doubt, read the conditions in their most obvious sense. Remember, however, that the language in the conditions is intended to be read for precise meaning. It is essential to pay particular attention to words that describe or limit relationships, such as "only," "exactly," "never," "always," "must be," "cannot be," and the like.

The result of this careful reading will be a clear picture of the structure of the relationships involved, including the kinds of relationships permitted, the participants in the relationships, and the range of possible actions or attributes for these participants.

Keep in mind question independence. Each question should be considered separately from the other questions in its set. No information, except what is given in the original conditions, should be carried over from one question to another.

In some cases a question will simply ask for conclusions to be drawn from the conditions as originally given. Some questions may, however, add information to the original conditions or temporarily suspend or replace one of the original conditions for the purpose of that question only. For example, if Question 1 adds the supposition "if P is sitting at table 2 ...," this supposition should NOT be carried over to any other question in the set.

Consider highlighting text and using diagrams. Many people find it useful to underline key points in the passage and in each question. In addition, it may prove very helpful to draw a diagram to assist you in finding the solution to the problem.

In preparing for the test, you may wish to experiment with different types of diagrams. For a scheduling problem, a simple calendar-like diagram may be helpful. For a grouping problem, an array of labeled columns or rows may be useful.

Even though most people find diagrams to be very helpful, some people seldom use them, and for some individual questions no one will need a diagram. There is by no means universal agreement on which kind of diagram is best for which problem or in which cases a diagram is most useful. Do not be concerned if a particular problem in the test seems to be best approached without the use of a diagram.

Logical Reasoning Questions

Arguments are a fundamental part of the law, and analyzing arguments is a key element of legal analysis. Training in the law builds on a foundation of basic reasoning skills. Law students must draw on the skills of analyzing, evaluating, constructing, and refuting arguments. They need to be able to identify what information is relevant to an issue or argument and what impact further evidence might have. They need to be able to reconcile opposing positions and use arguments to persuade others.

Logical Reasoning questions evaluate the ability to analyze, critically evaluate, and complete arguments as they occur in ordinary language. The questions are based on short arguments drawn from a wide variety of sources, including newspapers, general interest magazines, scholarly publications, advertisements, and informal discourse. These arguments mirror legal reasoning in the types of arguments presented and in their complexity, though few of the arguments actually have law as a subject matter.

Each Logical Reasoning question requires you to read and comprehend a short passage, then answer one question (or, rarely, two questions) about it. The questions are designed to assess a wide range of skills involved in thinking critically, with an emphasis on skills that are central to legal reasoning.

These skills include:

- Recognizing the parts of an argument and their relationships

- Recognizing similarities and differences between patterns of reasoning

- Drawing well-supported conclusions

- Reasoning by analogy

- Recognizing misunderstandings or points of disagreement

- Determining how additional evidence affects an argument

- Detecting assumptions made by particular arguments

- Identifying and applying principles or rules

- Identifying flaws in arguments

- Identifying explanations

The questions do not presuppose specialized knowledge of logical terminology. For example, you will not be expected to know the meaning of specialized terms such as "ad hominem" or "syllogism." On the other hand, you will be expected to understand and critique the reasoning contained in arguments. This requires that you possess a university-level understanding of widely used concepts such as argument, premise, assumption, and conclusion.

Suggested Approach

Read each question carefully. Make sure that you understand the meaning of each part of the question. Make sure that you understand the meaning of each answer choice and the ways in which it may or may not relate to the question posed.

Do not pick a response simply because it is a true statement. Although true, it may not answer the question posed.

Answer each question on the basis of the information that is given, even if you do not agree with it. Work within the context provided by the passage. LSAT questions do not involve any tricks or hidden meanings.

Reading Comprehension Questions

Both law school and the practice of law revolve around extensive reading of highly varied, dense, argumentative, and expository texts (for example, cases, codes, contracts, briefs, decisions, evidence). This reading must be exacting, distinguishing precisely what is said from what is not said. It involves comparison, analysis, synthesis, and application (for example, of principles and rules). It involves drawing appropriate inferences and applying ideas and arguments to new contexts. Law school reading also requires the ability to grasp unfamiliar subject matter and the ability to penetrate difficult and challenging material.

The purpose of LSAT Reading Comprehension questions is to measure the ability to read, with understanding and insight, examples of lengthy and complex materials similar to those commonly encountered in law school. The Reading Comprehension section of the LSAT contains four sets of reading questions, each set consisting of a selection of reading material followed by five to eight questions. The reading selection in three of the four sets consists of a single reading passage; the other set contains two related shorter passages. Sets with two passages are a variant of Reading Comprehension called Comparative Reading, which was introduced in June 2007.

Comparative Reading questions concern the relationships between the two passages, such as those of generalization/instance, principle/application, or point/counterpoint. Law school work often requires reading two or more texts in conjunction with each other and understanding their relationships. For example, a law student may read a trial court decision together with an appellate court decision that overturns it, or identify the fact pattern from a hypothetical suit together with the potentially controlling case law.

Reading selections for LSAT Reading Comprehension questions are drawn from a wide range of subjects in the humanities, the social sciences, the biological and physical sciences, and areas related to the law. Generally, the selections are densely written, use high-level vocabulary, and contain sophisticated argument or complex rhetorical structure (for example, multiple points of view). Reading Comprehension questions require you to read carefully and accurately, to determine the relationships among the various parts of the reading selection, and to draw reasonable inferences from the material in the selection. The questions may ask about the following characteristics of a passage or pair of passages:

- The main idea or primary purpose

- Information that is explicitly stated

- Information or ideas that can be inferred

- The meaning or purpose of words or phrases as used in context

- The organization or structure

- The application of information in the selection to a new context

- Principles that function in the selection

- Analogies to claims or arguments in the selection

- An author's attitude as revealed in the tone of a passage or the language used

- The impact of new information on claims or arguments in the selection

Suggested Approach

Since reading selections are drawn from many different disciplines and sources, you should not be discouraged if you encounter material with which you are not familiar. It is important to remember that questions are to be answered exclusively on the basis of the information provided in the selection. There is no particular knowledge that you are expected to bring to the test, and you should not make inferences based on any prior knowledge of a subject that you may have. You may, however, wish to defer working on a set of questions that seems particularly difficult or unfamiliar until after you have dealt with sets you find easier.

Strategies. One question that often arises in connection with Reading Comprehension has to do with the most effective and efficient order in which to read the selections and questions. Possible approaches include:

- reading the selection very closely and then answering the questions;

- reading the questions first, reading the selection closely, and then returning to the questions; or

- skimming the selection and questions very quickly, then rereading the selection closely and answering the questions.

Test takers are different, and the best strategy for one might not be the best strategy for another. In preparing for the test, therefore, you might want to experiment with the different strategies and decide what works most effectively for you.

Remember that your strategy must be effective under timed conditions. For this reason, the first strategy—reading the selection very closely and then answering the questions—may be the most effective for you. Nonetheless, if you believe that one of the other strategies

might be more effective for you, you should try it out and assess your performance using it.

Reading the selection. Whatever strategy you choose, you should give the passage or pair of passages at least one careful reading before answering the questions. Try to distinguish main ideas from supporting ideas, and opinions or attitudes from factual, objective information. Note transitions from one idea to the next and identify the relationships among the different ideas or parts of a passage, or between the two passages in Comparative Reading sets. Consider how and why an author makes points and draws conclusions. Be sensitive to implications of what the passages say.

You may find it helpful to mark key parts of passages. For example, you might underline main ideas or important arguments, and you might circle transitional words—"although," "nevertheless," "correspondingly," and the like—that will help you map the structure of a passage. Also, you might note descriptive words that will help you identify an author's attitude toward a particular idea or person.

Answering the Questions

- Always read all the answer choices before selecting the best answer. The best answer choice is the one that most accurately and completely answers the question being posed.

- Respond to the specific question being asked. Do not pick an answer choice simply because it is a true statement. For example, picking a true statement might yield an incorrect answer to a question in which you are asked to identify an author's position on an issue, since you are not being asked to evaluate the truth of the author's position but only to correctly identify what that position is.

- Answer the questions only on the basis of the information provided in the selection. Your own views, interpretations, or opinions, and those you have heard from others, may sometimes conflict with those expressed in a reading selection; however, you are expected to work within the context provided by the reading selection. You should not expect to agree with everything you encounter in Reading Comprehension passages.

THE WRITING SAMPLE

On the day of the test, you will be asked to write one sample essay. LSAC does not score the writing sample, but copies are sent to all law schools to which you apply. According to a 2015 LSAC survey of 129 United States and Canadian law schools, almost all use the writing sample in evaluating at least some applications for admission. Failure to respond to writing sample prompts and frivolous responses have been used by law schools as grounds for rejection of applications for admission.

In developing and implementing the writing sample portion of the LSAT, LSAC has operated on the following premises: First, law schools and the legal profession value highly the ability to communicate effectively in writing. Second, it is important to encourage potential law students to develop effective writing skills. Third, a sample of an applicant's writing, produced under controlled conditions, is a potentially useful indication of that person's writing ability. Fourth, the writing sample can serve as an independent check on other writing submitted by applicants as part of the admission process. Finally, writing samples may be useful for diagnostic purposes related to improving a candidate's writing.

The writing prompt presents a decision problem. You are asked to make a choice between two positions or courses of action. Both of the choices are defensible, and you are given criteria and facts on which to base your decision. There is no "right" or "wrong" position to take on the topic, so the quality of each test taker's response is a function not of which choice is made, but of how well or poorly the choice is supported and how well or poorly the other choice is criticized.

The LSAT writing prompt was designed and validated by legal education professionals. Since it involves writing based on fact sets and criteria, the writing sample gives applicants the opportunity to demonstrate the type of argumentative writing that is required in law school, although the topics are usually nonlegal.

You will have 35 minutes in which to plan and write an essay on the topic you receive. Read the topic and the accompanying directions carefully. You will probably find it best to spend a few minutes considering the topic and organizing your thoughts before you begin writing. In your essay, be sure to develop your ideas fully, leaving time, if possible, to review what you have written. Do not write on a topic other than the one specified. Writing on a topic of your own choice is not acceptable.

No special knowledge is required or expected for this writing exercise. Law schools are interested in the reasoning, clarity, organization, language usage, and writing mechanics displayed in your essay. How well you write is more important than how much you write. Confine your essay to the blocked, lined area on the front and back of the separate Writing Sample Response Sheet. Only that area will be reproduced for law schools. Be sure that your writing is legible.

TAKING THE PREPTEST UNDER SIMULATED LSAT CONDITIONS

One important way to prepare for the LSAT is to simulate the day of the test by taking a practice test under actual time constraints. Taking a practice test under timed conditions helps you to estimate the amount of time you can afford to spend on each question in a section and to determine the question types on which you may need additional practice.

Since the LSAT is a timed test, it is important to use your allotted time wisely. During the test, you may work only on the section designated by the test supervisor. You cannot devote extra time to a difficult section and make up that time on a section you find easier. In pacing yourself, and checking your answers, you should think of each section of the test as a separate minitest.

Be sure that you answer every question on the test. When you do not know the correct answer to a question, first eliminate the responses that you know are incorrect, then make your best guess among the remaining choices. Do not be afraid to guess as there is no penalty for incorrect answers.

When you take a practice test, abide by all the requirements specified in the directions and keep strictly within the specified time limits. Work without a rest period. When you take an actual test, you will have only a short break—usually 10–15 minutes—after SECTION III.

When taken under conditions as much like actual testing conditions as possible, a practice test provides very useful preparation for taking the LSAT.

Official directions for the four multiple-choice sections and the writing sample are included in this PrepTest so that you can approximate actual testing conditions as you practice.

To take the test:

- Set a timer for 35 minutes. Answer all the questions in SECTION I of this PrepTest. Stop working on that section when the 35 minutes have elapsed.

- Repeat, allowing yourself 35 minutes each for sections II, III, and IV.

- Set the timer again for 35 minutes, then prepare your response to the writing sample topic at the end of this PrepTest.

- Refer to "Computing Your Score" for the PrepTest for instruction on evaluating your performance. An answer key is provided for that purpose.

The practice test that follows consists of four sections corresponding to the four scored sections of the June 2015 LSAT. Also reprinted is the June 2015 unscored writing sample topic.

General Directions for the LSAT Answer Sheet

The actual testing time for this portion of the test will be 2 hours 55 minutes. There are five sections, each with a time limit of 35 minutes. The supervisor will tell you when to begin and end each section. If you finish a section before time is called, you may check your work on that section **only;** do not turn to any other section of the test book and do not work on any other section either in the test book or on the answer sheet.

There are several different types of questions on the test, and each question type has its own directions. **Be sure you understand the directions for each question type before attempting to answer any questions in that section.**

Not everyone will finish all the questions in the time allowed. Do not hurry, but work steadily and as quickly as you can without sacrificing accuracy. You are advised to use your time effectively. If a question seems too difficult, go on to the next one and return to the difficult question after completing the section. **MARK THE BEST ANSWER YOU CAN FOR EVERY QUESTION. NO DEDUCTIONS WILL BE MADE FOR WRONG ANSWERS. YOUR SCORE WILL BE BASED ONLY ON THE NUMBER OF QUESTIONS YOU ANSWER CORRECTLY.**

ALL YOUR ANSWERS MUST BE MARKED ON THE ANSWER SHEET. Answer spaces for each question are lettered to correspond with the letters of the potential answers to each question in the test book. After you have decided which of the answers is correct, blacken the corresponding space on the answer sheet. **BE SURE THAT EACH MARK IS BLACK AND COMPLETELY FILLS THE ANSWER SPACE.** Give only one answer to each question. If you change an answer, be sure that all previous marks are **erased completely.** Since the answer sheet is machine scored, incomplete erasures may be interpreted as intended answers. **ANSWERS RECORDED IN THE TEST BOOK WILL NOT BE SCORED.**

There may be more question numbers on this answer sheet than there are questions in a section. Do not be concerned, but be certain that the section and number of the question you are answering matches the answer sheet section and question number. Additional answer spaces in any answer sheet section should be left blank. Begin your next section in the number one answer space for that section.

LSAC takes various steps to ensure that answer sheets are returned from test centers in a timely manner for processing. In the unlikely event that an answer sheet is not received, LSAC will permit the examinee either to retest at no additional fee or to receive a refund of his or her LSAT fee. **THESE REMEDIES ARE THE ONLY REMEDIES AVAILABLE IN THE UNLIKELY EVENT THAT AN ANSWER SHEET IS NOT RECEIVED BY LSAC.**

Score Cancellation

Complete this section only if you are absolutely certain you want to cancel your score. **A CANCELLATION REQUEST CANNOT BE RESCINDED. IF YOU ARE AT ALL UNCERTAIN, YOU SHOULD NOT COMPLETE THIS SECTION.**

To cancel your score from this administration, you **must:**

A. fill in both ovals here ...... ◯ ◯

   AND

B. read the following statement. Then sign your name and enter the date.
   YOUR SIGNATURE ALONE IS NOT SUFFICIENT FOR SCORE CANCELLATION. BOTH OVALS ABOVE MUST BE FILLED IN FOR SCANNING EQUIPMENT TO RECOGNIZE YOUR REQUEST FOR SCORE CANCELLATION.

I certify that I wish to cancel my test score from this administration. I understand that my request is irreversible and that my score will not be sent to me or to the law schools to which I apply.

_____
Sign your name in full

_____
Date

FOR LSAC USE ONLY ⬤

HOW DID YOU PREPARE FOR THE LSAT?
(Select all that apply.)

Responses to this item are voluntary and will be used for statistical research purposes only.

◯ By studying the free sample questions available on LSAC's website.
◯ By taking the free sample LSAT available on LSAC's website.
◯ By working through official LSAT *PrepTests*, *ItemWise*, and/or other LSAC test prep products.
◯ By using LSAT prep books or software **not** published by LSAC.
◯ By attending a commercial test preparation or coaching course.
◯ By attending a test preparation or coaching course offered through an undergraduate institution.
◯ Self study.
◯ Other preparation.
◯ No preparation.

CERTIFYING STATEMENT

Please write the following statement. Sign and date.

I certify that I am the examinee whose name appears on this answer sheet and that I am here to take the LSAT for the sole purpose of being considered for admission to law school. I further certify that I will neither assist nor receive assistance from any other candidate, and I agree not to copy, retain, or transmit examination questions in any form or discuss them with any other person.

_____
_____
_____
_____
_____
_____
_____
_____
_____

SIGNATURE: _____ TODAY'S DATE: ____/____/____
                                                         MONTH DAY YEAR

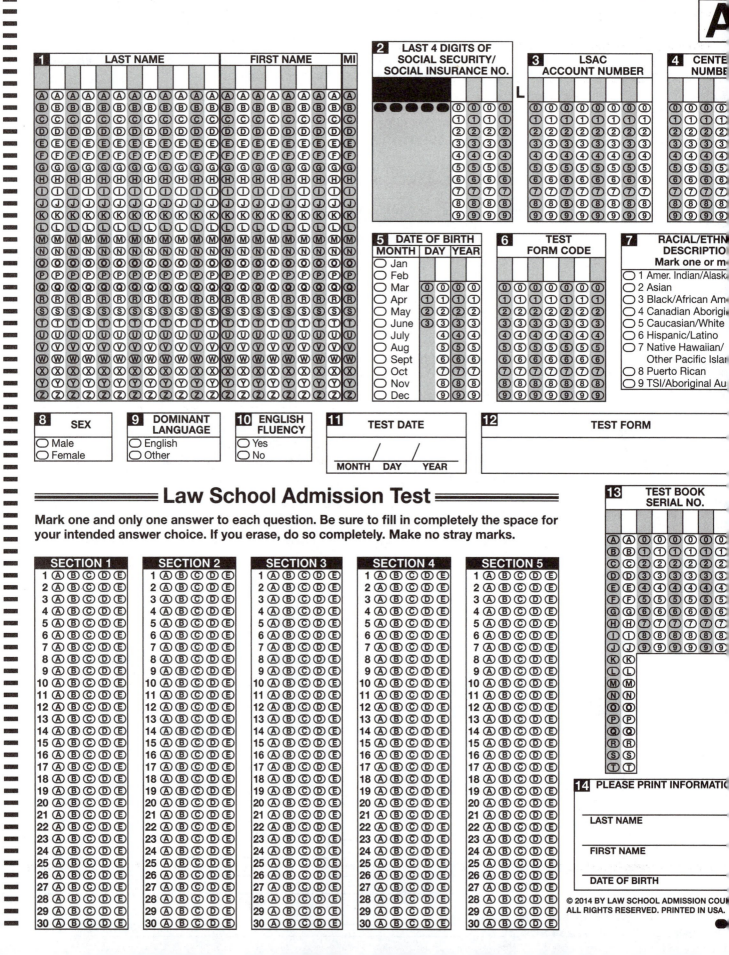

THE PREPTEST

SECTION I

Time—35 minutes

25 Questions

Directions: The questions in this section are based on the reasoning contained in brief statements or passages. For some questions, more than one of the choices could conceivably answer the question. However, you are to choose the best answer; that is, the response that most accurately and completely answers the question. You should not make assumptions that are by commonsense standards implausible, superfluous, or incompatible with the passage. After you have chosen the best answer, blacken the corresponding space on your answer sheet.

1. Pundit: Our city made a mistake when it sold a private company the rights to assess and collect parking fees. The private company raised parking fees and so has been able to reap profits far greater than what it paid for the rights to assess and collect the fees. If the city had not sold the rights, then that money would have gone to the city.

The pundit's argument requires the assumption that

(A) other private companies would have been willing to pay for the rights to assess and collect parking fees

(B) the city could have raised parking fees had it not sold the rights

(C) municipal functions like assessing and collecting parking fees should always be handled directly by the municipality in question

(D) the revenue from parking fees is not the only factor that cities need to consider in setting the rates for parking fees

(E) private companies assess and collect parking fees more efficiently than cities do

2. Popular science publications that explain new developments in science face a dilemma. In order to reach a wide audience, these publications must rely heavily on metaphorical writing, which usually fails to convey the science accurately. If the writing is more rigorous, they get the science right but fail to reach a wide audience. These publications should therefore give up trying to explain new developments in science to a wide audience.

Which one of the following principles, if valid, most helps to justify the reasoning in the argument?

(A) Science publications should balance the use of metaphors with more rigorous writing.

(B) The more recent a scientific development is, the harder it is to explain it accurately to a wide audience.

(C) In reporting scientific developments, it is better to fail to reach a wide audience than to be inaccurate.

(D) In reporting scientific developments, it is better to reach a wide audience than to be accurate.

(E) Even the most rigorous explanations of some scientific concepts must still contain metaphors.

GO ON TO THE NEXT PAGE.

3. Critic: Rock music is musically bankrupt and socially destructive, but at least the album covers of rock LPs from the 1960s and 1970s often featured innovative visual art. But now, since the success of digital music has almost ended the production of LPs, rock music has nothing going for it.

Which one of the following is an assumption on which the critic's argument relies?

(A) Digital music is not distributed with accompanying innovative visual art.
(B) Although very few LPs are produced today, most of these are rock LPs.
(C) In the 1960s and 1970s, only rock LPs featured innovative album cover art.
(D) The LPs being produced today have innovative album cover art.
(E) Rock music is less sophisticated musically and more destructive socially now than it was in the 1960s and 1970s.

4. Scientist: In testing whether a baby's babbling is a linguistic task or just random sounds, researchers videotaped the mouths of babies as they babbled. They discovered that babbling babies open the right sides of their mouths wider than the left. Past studies have established that during nonlinguistic vocalizations people generally open the left side of the mouth wider. So babbling turns out to be a linguistic task.

Which one of the following most accurately describes how the scientist's argument proceeds?

(A) It describes an argument for a given conclusion and presents a counterargument to suggest that its conclusion is incorrect.
(B) It questions the adequacy of a generally accepted principle by providing evidence to undermine that principle, and offers a different principle in its place.
(C) It raises a question, describes a potential experimental test, and argues that the test is necessary to answer the question.
(D) It describes an explanation for some facts, counters assertions that the explanation is unlikely to be correct, and concludes that it is correct after all.
(E) It presents two possible interpretations of a phenomenon and provides evidence in support of one interpretation and against the other.

5. Environment minister: Because of our concern about global warming, this country has committed itself to reducing its emissions of carbon dioxide substantially over the next ten years. Since trees absorb carbon dioxide, planting large numbers of trees will help us fulfill our commitment.

Which one of the following, if true, would most weaken the environment minister's argument?

(A) Owners of large tracts of private land are usually unwilling to plant trees unless they are given a financial incentive for doing so.
(B) Over the last ten years the proportion of land that is deforested annually has not increased as much as has the proportion of carbon dioxide in the atmosphere.
(C) When ground is disturbed in the course of planting trees, more carbon dioxide is released into the atmosphere by rotting organic matter in the soil than the new trees will absorb in ten years.
(D) Many climate researchers believe that global warming is such an urgent problem that carbon dioxide emissions should be substantially reduced in less than ten years.
(E) Gases other than carbon dioxide contribute to global warming, and trees do not absorb any of these other gases.

6. Sport utility vehicles (SUVs) are, because of their weight, extremely expensive to operate but, for the same reason, in an accident they are safer for their occupants than smaller vehicles are. Nonetheless, an analysis of recent traffic fatality statistics has led auto safety experts to conclude that the increasing popularity of SUVs is an alarming trend.

Which one of the following, if true, most helps to account for the response of auto safety experts to the popularity of SUVs?

(A) Vehicles with a reputation for being safer than others tend to be driven more carefully than other vehicles.
(B) Vehicles with a high average fuel consumption have fuel tanks with larger capacities.
(C) Recent statistics suggest that large vehicles such as SUVs tend to carry more passengers than smaller vehicles do.
(D) Recent statistics suggest that the average number of fatalities in collisions between SUVs and smaller vehicles is higher than for other collisions.
(E) Recent statistics suggest that SUVs are as likely to be involved in collisions as smaller vehicles are.

7. Political advertisement: Sherwood campaigns as an opponent of higher taxes. But is anybody fooled? For the last 10 years, while Sherwood served on the city council, the council consistently increased taxes year after year. Break the cycle of higher and higher taxes: reject Sherwood's bid for reelection to city council.

The argument in the political advertisement is most vulnerable to criticism on the grounds that it

(A) bases a crucial generalization on a very limited sample
(B) fails to consider the possibility that something that is unavoidable might nonetheless be undesirable
(C) mistakes something that is sufficient to bring about a result for something that is necessary to bring about that result
(D) makes a personal attack on someone who holds a certain view rather than addressing the reasonableness of that view
(E) takes for granted that a characteristic of a group as a whole is shared by an individual member of that group

8. Client: The owners of the catering company we use decided to raise their rates. They argued that the increase was necessary to allow them to hire and train new staff to accommodate their expanding client base. They should reconsider that decision and not raise their rates. After all, the mission of the company is to provide low-cost gourmet catering, and this mission will be jeopardized if they raise rates.

Which one of the following most accurately expresses the main conclusion of the client's argument?

(A) The owners of the catering company decided to raise their rates.
(B) The catering company needs to increase its rates to accommodate its expanding client base.
(C) The catering company's rates should not be raised.
(D) The catering company's mission is to provide low-cost gourmet catering.
(E) The catering company's mission will be jeopardized if its rates are increased.

9. Red admiral butterflies fly in a highly irregular fashion, constantly varying their speed, wing strokes, and flight path. While predators avoid poisonous butterfly species, nonpoisonous butterflies like the red admiral need to elude predators to survive. Scientists therefore hypothesize that the red admiral's flight style, which is clearly not energy efficient, evolved as a means of avoiding predators.

Which one of the following, if true, most strengthens the support for the scientists' hypothesis?

(A) No species of poisonous butterfly has an irregular flight style like that of the red admiral.
(B) Attacks from predators are not the most common cause of death for butterflies.
(C) Many other types of butterfly have flight styles similar to that of the red admiral.
(D) It is much more energy efficient for butterflies to fly in an irregular fashion than it is for heavier varieties of insects.
(E) All of the predators that prey on the red admiral also prey on other species of nonpoisonous butterflies.

10. Copyright statutes benefit society by providing incentive to produce original works, so some kind of copyright statute is ultimately justified. But these statutes also represent a significant cost to society because they create protected monopolies. In many countries, copyright statutes grant copyright protection for the life of the author plus several decades. This is too long, since the societal benefit from the additional years of copyright is more than offset by the societal cost.

Which one of the following principles, if valid, most strongly supports the reasoning in the argument?

(A) A statute should be written in a way that eliminates any appearance of its being inconsistent in its aims.
(B) A statute should be repealed if the conditions that originally justified enacting the statute no longer hold true.
(C) A statute that is justified in one country is justified in every country.
(D) A statute should not limit rights unless it can be shown that it thereby enhances other rights.
(E) If a statute is to be justified by its benefit to society, it should be designed so that its societal benefit always exceeds its societal cost.

GO ON TO THE NEXT PAGE.

11. Police chief: During my tenure as chief, crime in this city has fallen by 20 percent. This is clearly the result of my policing strategy, which uses real-time crime data and focuses police resources on the areas with the most crime.

Which one of the following, if true, most calls into question the police chief's explanation for the drop in crime?

(A) The crime rate in the police chief's city is still significantly higher than in many other cities.

(B) The crime rate in the police chief's city is higher now than it was several decades before the chief's tenure began.

(C) The crime rate in the police chief's city fell significantly during the first few years of the chief's tenure, then it leveled off.

(D) The crime rate in the country as a whole fell by about 30 percent during the police chief's tenure.

(E) The variation in crime rates between different areas of the city is smaller in the police chief's city than in many other cities.

12. Commentator: The Duke of Acredia argued long ago that only virtuous Acredian rulers concerned with the well-being of the people will be able to rule successfully. Since then, when Acredian governments have fallen, their falls have always been during the rule of one who viciously disregards the people's needs. The Duke, then, was right about at least one thing: Concern for the welfare of the people is necessary for the successful governance of Acredia.

The reasoning in the commentator's argument is most vulnerable to criticism on the grounds that the argument

(A) ignores the possibility that the conditions that are necessary for the welfare of the people are likely to change over time

(B) infers the necessity of a certain condition for success from the fact that its absence has always led to failure

(C) appeals to evidence from sources that are likely to be in some way biased or unreliable

(D) infers that a certain condition is required for success from the fact that the lack of that condition is associated with failure

(E) presumes, without providing justification, that the character of past rulers can be assessed in some completely objective way

13. Dr. Khan: Professor Burns recognizes that recent observations fail to confirm earlier ones that apparently showed a comet reservoir far out in our solar system. She claims this nonconfirmation is enough to show that the earlier observations are incorrect. But the recent observations occurred under poor conditions.

Which one of the following is most supported by Dr. Khan's statements?

(A) If the recent observations had been made under good conditions, they would have provided conclusive evidence of a comet reservoir far out in our solar system.

(B) Contrary to Professor Burns's view, the recent observations confirm the earlier ones.

(C) Professor Burns's claim about the implications of the recent observations is incorrect.

(D) The recent observations, even if they had been made under good conditions, would not have been enough to suggest that the earlier ones are incorrect.

(E) The poor conditions present during recent observations render them worthless.

14. If people refrained from being impolite to one another the condition of society would be greatly improved. But society would not be better off if the government enacted laws requiring people to be polite to each other. Enforcing such laws would create even more problems than does impoliteness.

Which one of the following most accurately describes the role played in the argument by the claim that society would not be better off if the government enacted laws requiring people to be polite to each other?

(A) It is the conclusion drawn by the argument as a whole.

(B) It is cited as evidence for the generalization that is the argument's overall conclusion.

(C) It is cited as evidence for the assertion used to support the argument's overall conclusion.

(D) It is cited as an illustration of a generalization that serves as the main premise of the argument.

(E) It describes a phenomenon that the conclusion of the argument purports to explain.

GO ON TO THE NEXT PAGE.

15. Astronomer: In most cases in which a planet has been detected orbiting a distant star, the planet's orbit is distinctly oval, whereas the orbits of Earth and several other planets around our sun are approximately circular. However, many comets orbiting our sun have been thrown into oval orbits by close encounters with planets orbiting our sun. So some of the planets in oval orbits around distant stars were probably thrown into those orbits by close encounters with other planets orbiting the same stars.

Which one of the following, if true, would most strengthen the astronomer's argument?

(A) When two planets or other large objects in orbit have a close encounter, usually the smaller of the two is the more greatly affected.

(B) There is no indication that the orbit of any planet orbiting our sun has been affected by a close encounter with another planet orbiting our sun.

(C) In most cases in which planets have been discovered orbiting a distant star, more than one planet has been found orbiting the star.

(D) Most comets with an oval orbit around our sun were thrown into that orbit by a close encounter with some other object.

(E) For each distant star that has been found to have a planet, no other object large enough to affect the planet's orbit has been found orbiting the star.

16. It is possible to grow agricultural crops that can thrive when irrigated with seawater. Such farming, if undertaken near oceans, would actually be cheaper than most other irrigated agriculture, since the water would not have to be pumped far. The greatest expense in irrigated agriculture is in pumping the water, and the pumping costs increase with the distance the water is pumped.

Which one of the following most accurately describes the role played in the argument by the claim that the greatest expense in irrigated agriculture is in pumping the water?

(A) It is a claim that the argument shows to be false.

(B) It is a hypothesis that, if proven, would undermine the argument's conclusion.

(C) It is evidence provided to support the argument's conclusion.

(D) It is the argument's conclusion.

(E) It is a claim for which the argument provides evidence, but which is not the argument's conclusion.

17. Critics worry that pessimistic news reports about the economy harm it by causing people to lose confidence in the economy, of which everyone has direct experience every day. Journalists respond that to do their jobs well they cannot worry about the effects of their work. Also, studies show that people do not defer to journalists except on matters of which they have no direct experience.

The statements above, if true, most strongly support which one of the following?

(A) Critics who think that the economy is affected by the extent of people's confidence in it are wrong.

(B) Pessimistic news reports about such matters as foreign policy, of which people do not have experience every day, are likely to have a negative impact.

(C) Pessimistic news reports about the state of the economy are likely to harm the economy.

(D) News reports about the economy are unlikely to have a significant effect on people's opinions about the state of the economy.

(E) Journalists need not be deeply concerned about their reporting's effects on the well-being of the average citizen.

18. Police captain: The chief of police has indicated that gifts of cash or objects valued at more than $100 count as graft. However, I know with certainty that no officer in my precinct has ever taken such gifts, so the recent accusations of graft in my precinct are unfounded.

The reasoning in the police captain's argument is most vulnerable to criticism on the grounds that the argument

(A) bases a rebuttal of accusations of graft on knowledge about only a limited sample of officers

(B) fails to consider that there may be other instances of graft besides those indicated by the chief of police

(C) bases a claim about the actions of individuals on an appeal to the character of those individuals

(D) takes for granted that if the accusations of graft are unfounded, so is any accusation of corruption

(E) relies on a premise that contradicts the conclusion drawn in the argument

GO ON TO THE NEXT PAGE.

19. Economist: Although average hourly wages vary considerably between different regions of this country, in each region, the average hourly wage for full-time jobs increased last year. Paradoxically, however, in the country as a whole, the average hourly wage for full-time jobs decreased last year.

Which one of the following, if true of the economist's country, most helps to resolve the apparent paradox in the economist's statements?

(A) In the country as a whole, the average hourly wage for full-time jobs has decreased slightly for each of the last three years.

(B) Last year, to reduce costs, employers moved many full-time jobs from regions with relatively high hourly wages to regions where those jobs typically pay much less.

(C) The year before last, the unemployment rate reached a ten-year low; last year, however, the unemployment rate increased slightly.

(D) Last year, the rate at which the average hourly wage for full-time jobs increased varied considerably between different regions of the country.

(E) Last year, hourly wages for most full-time jobs in the manufacturing sector declined while those for most full-time jobs in the service sector increased.

20. Researchers compared the brains of recently deceased people who had schizophrenia with those of recently deceased people who did not have schizophrenia. They found that 35 percent of the former and none of the latter showed evidence of damage to a structure of nerve cells called the subplate. They knew that this damage must have occurred prior to the second fetal trimester, when the subplate controls the development of the connections between the different parts of the brain.

Which one of the following conclusions is most strongly supported by the information above?

(A) Roughly 35 percent of people with abnormal brain subplates will eventually have schizophrenia.

(B) A promising treatment in some cases of schizophrenia is repair of the damaged connections between the different parts of the brain.

(C) Some people developed schizophrenia because of damage to the brain subplate after the second fetal trimester.

(D) Schizophrenia is determined by genetic factors.

(E) There may be a cause of schizophrenia that predates birth.

21. A new device uses the global positioning system to determine a cow's location and, when a cow strays outside of its pasture, makes noises in the cow's ears to steer it back to its home range. Outfitting all of the cattle in a herd with this device is far more expensive than other means of keeping cattle in their pastures, such as fences. The device's maker nevertheless predicts that ranchers will purchase the device at its current price.

Which one of the following, if true, does the most to support the prediction made by the device's maker?

(A) The price of the device will come down appreciably if the device's maker is able to produce it in large quantities.

(B) As they graze, cattle in a herd follow the lead of the same few members of the herd.

(C) The device has been shown not to cause significant stress to cattle.

(D) The device has been shown to be as effective as fences at keeping cattle in their pastures.

(E) The device's maker offers significant discounts to purchasers who buy in bulk.

GO ON TO THE NEXT PAGE.

22. Food co-ops are a type of consumer cooperative. Consumer cooperatives offer the same products as other stores but usually more cheaply. It is therefore more economical to shop at a food co-op than at a supermarket.

Which one of the following is most appropriate as an analogy demonstrating that the reasoning in the argument above is flawed?

(A)   By that line of reasoning, we could conclude that people who own sports cars use much more gasoline in their cars than people who own other types of cars, since sports cars use more gasoline per mile than most other cars.

(B)   By that line of reasoning, we could conclude that it is better to buy frozen vegetables than fresh vegetables, since fresh vegetables are more expensive than frozen vegetables and spoil more quickly.

(C)   By that line of reasoning, we could conclude that a person who rides a bicycle causes more pollution per mile traveled than one who rides a public bus, since bicycling is a private means of transportation and private means of transportation tend to generate more pollution per mile traveled than do public means.

(D)   By that line of reasoning, we could conclude that more people must be shopping at health food stores than ever before, since people tend to choose healthful food over unhealthful food as long as the healthful food tastes at least as good, and healthful food today is better tasting than ever.

(E)   By that line of reasoning, we could conclude that the best way to lose weight is to increase one's consumption of artificially sweetened foods, since artificially sweetened foods have fewer calories than foods sweetened with sugar, and excessive calorie intake contributes to weight gain.

23. Editorial: The gates at most railroad crossings, while they give clear warning of oncoming trains, are not large enough to prevent automobile drivers from going around them onto the tracks. Some people claim that the ensuing accidents are partly the fault of the railroad company, but this is a mistake. Granted, if one has a small child in the house, then one ought to block access to stairs completely; but a licensed driver is a capable adult who should know better.

The editorial's conclusion follows logically if which one of the following is assumed?

(A)   The gates could be made larger, yet irresponsible drivers might still be able to go around them onto the tracks.

(B)   Capable adults have a responsibility to take some measures to ensure their own safety.

(C)   When the warnings of companies are disregarded by capable adults, the adults are fully responsible for any resulting accidents.

(D)   Small children are not involved in accidents resulting from drivers going around the gates.

(E)   Any company's responsibility to promote public safety is not unlimited.

GO ON TO THE NEXT PAGE.

24. Researcher: People who participate in opinion surveys often give answers they believe the opinion surveyor expects to hear, and it is for this reason that some opinion surveys do not reflect the actual views of those being surveyed. However, in well-constructed surveys, the questions are worded so as to provide respondents with no indication of which answers the surveyor might expect. So if a survey is well constructed, survey respondents' desire to meet surveyors' expectations has no effect on the survey's results.

The reasoning in the researcher's argument is questionable in that the argument overlooks the possibility that

(A) an opinion survey that disguises the surveyor's expectations may be flawed in a number of ways, some of which have nothing to do with the surveyor's expectations

(B) when people who respond to opinion surveys hold strong opinions, their answers are unlikely to be influenced by other people's expectations

(C) many opinion surveyors have no expectations whatsoever regarding the answers of people who respond to surveys

(D) some people who know what answers an opinion surveyor expects to hear will purposefully try to thwart the surveyor's expectations

(E) the answers of opinion-survey respondents can be influenced by beliefs about the surveyor's expectations even if those beliefs are unfounded

25. The availability of television reduces the amount of reading children do. When television is made unavailable, a nearly universal increase in reading, both by parents and by children, is reported. When television is available again, the level of reading by both parents and children relapses to its previous level.

The reasoning in which one of the following is most similar to the reasoning above?

(A) Whenever the money supply in an economy fluctuates, interest rates tend to fluctuate. When the money supply remains constant, interest rates tend to remain stable. Thus, the money supply's remaining constant stabilizes interest rates.

(B) The consumption of candy between meals disrupts a child's appetite at mealtimes. When candy is not consumed, blood sugar declines until mealtime, so the child feels hungry. A child who eats healthy meals feels less desire for candy.

(C) Global warming is caused by increased carbon dioxide in the atmosphere. Furthermore, industrial pollution causes increased carbon dioxide in the atmosphere. So industrial pollution causes global warming.

(D) Voting behavior is affected by factors other than political candidates' records of political achievement. For example, a candidate who projects confidence will gain votes as a result, whereas a candidate with a supercilious facial expression will lose votes.

(E) Adults read less than they once did because there are so many other activities to divert them. This can be seen from the fact that the more time they spend on such other activities, the less they read. Conversely, the less they read, the more time they spend on such other activities.

S T O P

IF YOU FINISH BEFORE TIME IS CALLED, YOU MAY CHECK YOUR WORK ON THIS SECTION ONLY.
DO NOT WORK ON ANY OTHER SECTION IN THE TEST.

SECTION II

Time—35 minutes

27 Questions

<u>Directions:</u> Each set of questions in this section is based on a single passage or a pair of passages. The questions are to be answered on the basis of what is <u>stated</u> or <u>implied</u> in the passage or pair of passages. For some of the questions, more than one of the choices could conceivably answer the question. However, you are to choose the <u>best</u> answer; that is, the response that most accurately and completely answers the question, and blacken the corresponding space on your answer sheet.

Having spent several decades trying to eliminate the unself-conscious "colonial gaze" characteristic of so many early ethnographic films, visual anthropologists from the industrialized West who study indigenous
(5) cultures are presently struggling with an even more profound transformation of their discipline. Because inexpensive video equipment is now available throughout the world, many indigenous peoples who were once examined by the Western ethnographer's
(10) camera have begun to document their own cultures. Reaction to this phenomenon within Western anthropological circles is sharply divided.

One faction, led by anthropologist James Weiner, sees the proliferation of video and television as the
(15) final assault of Western values on indigenous cultures. Weiner argues that the spread of video represents "a devaluation of the different," culminating in the replacement of genuine historical, linguistic, social, and cultural difference with superficial difference
(20) among electronic images. He believes that video technologies inevitably purvey a Western ontology, one based on realism, immediacy, and self-expression. Thus, Weiner concludes, using video technology costs indigenous peoples the very cultural identity they seek
(25) to record. Moreover, he maintains that anthropologists who attribute a paramount truth value to these films simply because they are made by indigenous peoples are theoretically naive.

But Weiner's opponents contend that his views
(30) betray a certain nostalgia for the idea of the "noble savage." One such opponent, anthropologist Faye Ginsburg, concedes that no Western object that has entered cultural circulation since the fifteenth century has been neutral, but she considers it
(35) little more than boilerplate technological determinism to argue that using a video camera makes one unwittingly Western. Unlike Weiner, Ginsburg maintains that non-Western indigenous peoples can use Western media without adopting the conventions of Western
(40) culture. In fact, Ginsburg and many other anthropologists believe that video affords societies—especially oral ones—an invaluable opportunity to strengthen native languages and traditions threatened by Western exposure.

The Brazilian fieldwork of anthropologist
(45) Terence Turner, who studies the relationship between traditional Kayapo culture and Kayapo videotapes, lends credence to Ginsburg's position. Primarily an oral society, the Kayapo use video to document both ceremonial performances and transactions with
(50) representatives of the Brazilian government (this latter use is intended to provide legally binding records of

the transactions). In contrast to Weiner's argument that video foists a Western ontology onto its users, Turner has found that the representations of Kayapo
(55) ceremonies, including everything from the camerawork to the editing, conform to the same principle of beauty embodied in the ceremonies themselves, one rooted in a complex pattern of repetition and sequential organization. The videos aesthetically mirror the
(60) ceremonies. The camera is not so at odds with Kayapo culture, it seems, that it transforms any Kayapo who uses it into a Westerner.

1. Which one of the following most accurately and completely summarizes the passage?

(A) Some anthropologists argue that the proliferation of video technology has been harmful to indigenous peoples because it encourages the adoption of a Western ontology based on immediacy and self-expression.

(B) By making video technology available to indigenous peoples throughout the world, anthropologists have succeeded in eliminating the "colonial gaze" that many early ethnographic films exhibited.

(C) Anthropologists are divided in their assessments of the impact of video technology on indigenous peoples, but there is some evidence that video technology is compatible with the preservation of indigenous cultures.

(D) Some anthropologists argue that the proliferation of video technology has actually strengthened indigenous cultures threatened by Western influences, but the long-term impact of video technology on indigenous cultures is still unknown.

(E) The Kayapo people's use of video technology validates the position of one faction in the debate in anthropological circles regarding the effect of the proliferation of Western video technology on indigenous cultures.

GO ON TO THE NEXT PAGE.

2. Based on the passage, which one of the following most accurately describes Faye Ginsburg's stance toward the position attributed to James Weiner?

(A) fundamental rejection
(B) reluctant censure
(C) mild disapproval
(D) diplomatic neutrality
(E) supportive interest

3. Which one of the following is most analogous to the Kayapo's use of video to document ceremonial performances, as that use is described in the last paragraph?

(A) As various groups have emigrated to North America, they have brought their culinary traditions with them and thereby altered the culinary practices of North America.
(B) In the 1940s, Latin American composers incorporated African American inspired jazz instrumentation and harmonies into their music but remained faithful to the traditions of Latin American music.
(C) Some writers are predicting that the interactive nature of the Internet will fundamentally reshape fiction, and they are already producing narratives that take advantage of this capacity.
(D) In the late 1980s, some fashion designers produced lines of various articles of clothing that imitated fashions that were current in the 1920s and 1930s.
(E) Early in the twentieth century, some experimental European artists rejected the representational traditions of Western painting and began to produce works inspired by surrealist literature.

4. According to the passage, Weiner claims that an essential characteristic of Western ontology is

(A) a pattern of sequential organization
(B) paramount truth value
(C) self-expression
(D) the "colonial gaze"
(E) theoretical naivete

5. The passage provides information that is most helpful in answering which one of the following questions?

(A) Why do the Kayapo use video technology to create legal records?
(B) What is the origin of the idea of the "noble savage"?
(C) Which indigenous cultures have not yet adopted Western video technologies?
(D) Which Western technologies entered cultural circulation in the fifteenth century?
(E) What factors have made video equipment as inexpensive as it now is?

6. Terence Turner would be most likely to agree with which one of the following assessments of Weiner's position regarding the spread of video?

(A) Weiner fails to recognize the vast diversity of traditional practices among the world's indigenous peoples.
(B) Weiner overestimates the extent to which video technology has become available throughout the world.
(C) Weiner does not fully recognize the value of preserving the traditional practices of indigenous peoples.
(D) Weiner underestimates indigenous peoples' capacity for adapting the products of alien cultures to fit their own cultural values.
(E) Weiner ignores the fact that, even before the spread of video, many Western technologies had already been adapted by indigenous cultures.

7. In using the phrase "technological determinism" (line 35), the author refers to the idea that

(A) technology is exchanged in ways that appear to be predestined
(B) the technologies used by field anthropologists influence their views of the cultures they study
(C) cultures generally evolve in the direction of greater dependence on technology
(D) a culture's ethical values determine its reaction to new technologies
(E) cultures are shaped in fundamental ways by the technologies they use

GO ON TO THE NEXT PAGE.

The current approach to recusal and disqualification of judges heavily emphasizes appearance-based analysis. Professional codes of conduct for judges typically focus on the avoidance of both impropriety
(5) and the appearance of impropriety. Judges are expected to recuse (i.e., remove) themselves from any case in which their impartiality might reasonably be questioned. In some jurisdictions, statutes allow a party to a court proceeding to request disqualification of a judge for
(10) bias. In other jurisdictions, the responsibility for recusal falls upon the judge alone.

The rules provide vague guidance at best, making disqualification dependent on whether the judge's impartiality "might reasonably be questioned,"
(15) without giving any idea of whose perspective to take or how to interpret the facts. It is a mistake for rules governing judicial ethics to focus on the appearance of justice rather than on the elimination of bias that renders a judge cognitively incapable of properly
(20) reaching a just outcome because of a too-close personal involvement in the matter before the court. Focusing on appearances may cause sources of actual bias that are not apparent to outside observers, or even to judges themselves, to be overlooked.

(25) The function of the law is the settlement of normative disputes. Such settlement will work only if it is well reasoned. The achievement of actual justice by the use of legal reasoning is the primary function of judges. Therefore, the best way to address concerns
(30) about judicial impartiality is to require judges to make their reasoning transparent. Accordingly, we should eliminate disqualification motions alleging bias, whether actual or apparent. This unreliable mechanism should be replaced by the requirement of a written
(35) explanation of either the reasons for a judge's decision to recuse, or if the judge decides against recusal, the legal basis for the judgment reached, based on the merits of the case. That is, judges should not be required to explain why they did not recuse themselves,
(40) but rather they should be required to show the legal reasoning on the basis of which their ultimate judgments were made.

A potential objection is that the reasoning given by the judge, however legally adequate, may not be
(45) the judge's real reasoning, thus allowing for the presence of undetected bias. However, as long as a knowledgeable observer cannot find any fault with the legal reasoning provided, then there are no grounds for complaint. Under the law, a right of recourse arises only if harm
(50) accrues. If a judge who had no improper considerations in mind could have reached the same conclusion for the reasons stated by a judge who had hidden reasons in mind, then there is no harm on which to base a complaint.

8. According to the passage, a weakness of current rules regarding recusal and disqualification is that they

(A) interfere with judges' reasoning about the cases that they hear
(B) fail to specify whose perspective is relevant to determining apparent bias
(C) exaggerate the importance of transparency in judicial reasoning
(D) place responsibility for recusal entirely on judges
(E) ignore the importance of the appearance of propriety

9. Which one of the following most accurately expresses the primary purpose of the second paragraph?

(A) to state the author's objections to the approach described in the first paragraph
(B) to present a solution that is rejected in the third paragraph
(C) to provide concrete examples of the problems discussed in the first paragraph
(D) to explore the history that led to the situation described in the first paragraph
(E) to state the thesis to be defended in the rest of the passage

10. The author of the passage regards the legal principle that "a right of recourse arises only if harm accrues" (lines 49–50) as

(A) an established principle of law
(B) part of the definition of the function of the law
(C) a tool for judges to disguise their real reasoning
(D) unfair to parties to legal proceedings
(E) central to the current means of addressing judicial bias

GO ON TO THE NEXT PAGE.

11. It can be inferred from the passage that the author would be most likely to consider which one of the following to be a weakness of statutes that allow parties to court proceedings to request disqualification of judges for bias?

(A) The guidelines for applying such statutes are excessively rigid.

(B) Such statutes are incompatible with a requirement that judges make their reasoning transparent.

(C) Such statutes can fail to eliminate actual bias because parties to court proceedings are not always aware of judges' prejudices.

(D) Such statutes conflict with professional codes of conduct that require judges to recuse themselves if they believe that they are biased.

(E) There is no guarantee that all requests for disqualification of judges will be granted.

12. The passage suggests that if judges are required to provide written explanations for the legal reasoning underlying their decisions about cases, then

(A) judicial bias will be almost completely eliminated

(B) any faulty reasoning employed by judges can in principle be detected

(C) judges' written explanations will usually conceal their real reasoning

(D) the public perception of the impartiality of the judiciary will improve

(E) judges will be motivated to recuse themselves when there is an appearance of bias

13. Which one of the following would be an example of the kind of "real reasoning" referred to in the first sentence of the last paragraph of the passage?

(A) the reasoning leading to a judge's decision against recusal

(B) an argument that is too technical to be understood by someone without formal legal training

(C) reasoning that is motivated by the judge's personal animus against a defendant

(D) reasoning that a knowledgeable observer cannot find any fault with

(E) a central legal principle referred to in a judge's written explanation

14. The author would be most likely to consider which one of the following to be an accurate description of the effects of the current approach to recusal and disqualification of judges?

(A) The standards in place fail to assure the general public that the legal system is adequately protected against judicial bias.

(B) The professional codes of conduct for judges are considered meddlesome and ineffective by many judges.

(C) Judges are rarely removed from cases for bias when they are not actually biased, but they are allowed to sit on many cases even though they are biased.

(D) Judges are rarely allowed to sit on cases when they are biased, but judges are removed from many cases for bias even though they are not actually biased.

(E) Judges are sometimes removed from cases for bias even though they are not actually biased, while some instances of judicial bias occur and are never detected.

GO ON TO THE NEXT PAGE.

Passage A

Saint Augustine wrote that to proceed against lies by lying would be like countering robbery with robbery. To respond to wrongdoing by emulating it is certainly at times to accept lower standards.

(5)   And yet it has seemed to many that there is indeed some justification for repaying lies with lies. Such views go back as far as the kind of justice that demands an eye for an eye. They appeal to our sense of fairness: to lie to liars is to give them what they deserve, to

(10)   restore an equilibrium they themselves have upset. Just as bullies forfeit the right not to be interfered with by others, so liars forfeit the right to be dealt with honestly.

Two separate moral questions are involved in

(15)   this debate. The first asks whether a liar has the same claim to be told the truth as an honest person. The second asks whether one is more justified in lying to a liar than to others.

In order to see this distinction clearly, consider a

(20)   person known by all to be a pathological liar but quite harmless. Surely, as the idea of forfeiture suggests, the liar would have no cause for complaint if lied to. But his tall tales would not constitute sufficient reason to lie to him. For the harm to self, others, and general

(25)   trust that can come from the practice of lying has to be taken into account in weighing how to deal with him, not merely his personal characteristics.

Passage B

A view derived from Immanuel Kant holds that when rational beings act immorally toward others,

(30)   then, by virtue of their status as rational beings, they implicitly authorize similar actions as punishment aimed toward themselves. That is, acting rationally, one always acts as one would have others act toward oneself. Consequently, to act toward a person as that

(35)   person has acted toward others is to treat that person as a rational being, that is, as if that person's act is the product of a rational decision.

From this it might be concluded that we have a duty to do to offenders what they have done, since

(40)   this amounts to according them the respect due rational beings. But the assertion of a duty to punish seems excessive, since if this duty to others is necessary to accord them the respect due rational beings, then we would have a duty to do to all rational

(45)   persons everything—good, bad, or indifferent—that they do to others. The point is rather that by your acts and by virtue of your status as a rational being, you authorize others to do the same to you; you do not compel them to do so. The Kantian argument leads to

(50)   a right rather than a duty. Rational beings cannot validly object to being treated in the way in which they treated others. Where there is no valid complaint, there is no injustice, and where there is no injustice, others have acted within their rights.

15. Both passages are concerned with answering which one of the following questions?

   (A)   Can immoral actions be harmless?
   (B)   Should the same rules apply in evaluating moral wrongs and criminal wrongs?
   (C)   Is it right to respond to a person's wrongdoing with an action of the same kind?
   (D)   What is the difference between a duty and a right?
   (E)   Is it just to treat all wrongdoers as rational beings?

16. Which one of the following considerations is introduced in passage A but not in passage B?

   (A)   the harm that may result as a consequence of treating people as they treat others
   (B)   the consequences of not reciprocating another's wrongdoing
   (C)   the properties an action must have to count as rational
   (D)   the extent to which people who break moral rules are due respect
   (E)   instances in which people have been wronged by being treated as they treated others

17. The passages are alike in that each seeks to advance its main argument by

   (A)   anticipating and refuting the most probable objections to a theory
   (B)   using an analogy to support its overall claim
   (C)   focusing on a specific case to illustrate a generalization
   (D)   suggesting that a view can have unreasonable consequences
   (E)   offering and defending a new definition for a commonly used term

GO ON TO THE NEXT PAGE.

18. The author of passage A would be most likely to agree with which one of the following statements?

(A) Maintaining a policy of reciprocating wrongdoing fails to accord rational beings the respect that they are due.

(B) People have a duty to respond to even the morally neutral actions of others with actions of the same kind.

(C) It can be unjustified to treat a person in a certain way even though that person has forfeited the right not to be treated in that way.

(D) There is no circumstance in which there is sufficient reason to counter a wrong with a wrong of the same kind.

(E) To restore moral equilibrium, justice will occasionally require that an innocent person forfeit the right to be treated in a certain way.

19. Which one of the following most accurately characterizes the difference between the kind of right referred to in passage A (lines 11–13) and the kind of right referred to in passage B (line 50)?

(A) In passage A, the kind of right referred to is a legal right, whereas in passage B the kind of right referred to is a moral right.

(B) In passage A, the kind of right referred to involves benefits granted by society, whereas in passage B the kind of right referred to involves benefits granted by an individual in a position of authority.

(C) In passage A, the kind of right referred to is an entitlement held by groups of people, whereas in passage B the kind of right referred to is an entitlement held only by individuals.

(D) In passage A, the kind of right referred to is something that cannot be given up, whereas in passage B the kind of right referred to is something that can be lost because of certain actions.

(E) In passage A, the kind of right referred to involves behavior that one is entitled to from others, whereas in passage B the kind of right referred to involves behavior that one is licensed to engage in.

20. Which one of the following, if true, would most help to make the suggestion in passage A that a harmless pathological liar's tall tales would not constitute sufficient reason to lie to him (lines 23–24) compatible with the Kantian argument laid out in the first paragraph of passage B?

(A) Responding to pathological behavior with pathological behavior is irrational.

(B) Rationality cannot be reasonably attributed to pathological behavior.

(C) Pathological liars, if harmless, deserve to be treated as rational beings by others.

(D) Having the right to lie to a pathological liar is not equivalent to having a duty to do so.

(E) To model one's behavior on that of a pathological liar is to lower one's own standards.

GO ON TO THE NEXT PAGE.

To glass researchers it seems somewhat strange that many people throughout the world share the persistent belief that window glass flows slowly downward like a very viscous liquid. Repeated in
(5) reference books, in science classes, and elsewhere, the idea has often been invoked to explain ripply windows in old houses. The origins of the myth are unclear, but the confusion probably arose partly from a misunderstanding of the fact that the atoms in glass
(10) are not arranged in a fixed crystal structure. In this respect, the structure of liquid glass and the structure of solid glass are very similar, but thermodynamically they are not the same. Glass does not have a precise freezing point; rather, it has what is known as a glass
(15) transition temperature, typically a range of a few hundred degrees Celsius. Cooled below the lower end of this range, molten glass retains an amorphous atomic structure, but it takes on the physical properties of a solid.
(20) However, a new study debunks the persistent belief that stained glass windows in medieval cathedrals are noticeably thicker at the bottom because the glass flows downward. Under the force of gravity, certain solid materials including glass can, in fact, flow
(25) slightly. But Brazilian researcher Edgar Dutra Zanotto has calculated the time needed for viscous flow to change the thickness of different types of glass by a noticeable amount, and, according to his calculations, medieval cathedral glass would require a period well
(30) beyond the age of the universe.
The chemical composition of the glass determines the rate of flow. Even germanium oxide glass, which flows more easily than other types, would take many trillions of years to sag noticeably, Zanotto calculates.
(35) Medieval stained glass contains impurities that could lower the viscosity and speed the flow to some degree, but even a significant difference in this regard would not alter the conclusion, since the cathedrals are only several hundred years old. The study demonstrates
(40) dramatically what many scientists had reasoned earlier based on information such as the fact that for glass to have more than a negligible ability to flow, it would have to be heated to at least 350 degrees Celsius.
The difference in thickness sometimes observed
(45) in antique windows probably results instead from glass manufacturing methods. Until the nineteenth century, the only way to make window glass was to blow molten glass into a large globe and then flatten it into a disk. Whirling the disk introduced ripples and
(50) thickened the edges. To achieve structural stability, it would have made sense to install these panes in such a way that the thick portions were at the bottom. Later, glass was drawn into sheets by pulling it from the melt on a rod, a method that made windows more
(55) uniform. Today, most window glass is made by floating liquid glass on molten tin. This process makes the surface extremely flat.

21. Which one of the following most accurately states the main point of the passage?

(A) Zanotto's research has proven that the amount of time required for viscous flow to change the thickness of medieval cathedral glass would be greater than the age of the universe.

(B) The technology of window-glass production has progressed substantially from medieval stained-glass techniques to today's production of very flat and very uniform panes.

(C) After years of investigation motivated partly by a common misunderstanding about the structure of glass, scientists have developed ways of precisely calculating even extremely slow rates of gravity-induced flow in solids such as glass.

(D) Recent research provides evidence that although solid glass flows slightly under the influence of gravity, such flow is only one of several factors that have contributed to noticeable differences in thickness between the top and the bottom of some old windows.

(E) Contrary to a commonly held belief, noticeable differences in thickness between the top and the bottom of some old glass windows are not due to the flowing of solid glass, but probably result instead from old glassworking techniques.

22. The passage most helps to answer which one of the following questions?

(A) What is one way in which seventeenth-century windowpane manufacturing techniques differ from those commonly used in medieval times?

(B) What is one way in which nineteenth-century windowpane manufacturing techniques differ from those commonly used today?

(C) Was glass ever used in windows prior to medieval times?

(D) Are unevenly thick stained-glass windowpanes ever made of germanium oxide glass?

(E) How did there come to be impurities in medieval stained glass?

GO ON TO THE NEXT PAGE.

23. Which one of the following best summarizes the author's view of the results of Zanotto's study?

(A) They provide some important quantitative data to support a view that was already held by many scientists.

(B) They have stimulated important new research regarding an issue that scientists previously thought had been settled.

(C) They offer a highly plausible explanation of how a mistaken hypothesis came to be widely believed.

(D) They provide a conceptual basis for reconciling two scientific views that were previously thought to be incompatible.

(E) They suggest that neither of two hypotheses adequately explains a puzzling phenomenon.

24. The passage suggests that the atomic structure of glass is such that glass will

(A) behave as a liquid even though it has certain properties of solids

(B) be noticeably deformed by the force of its own weight over a period of a few millennia

(C) behave as a solid even when it has reached its glass transition temperature

(D) flow downward under its own weight if it is heated to its glass transition temperature

(E) stop flowing only if the atoms are arranged in a fixed crystalline structure

25. The author of the passage attributes the belief that window glass flows noticeably downward over time to the erroneous assumption that

(A) the atomic structure of solid glass is crystalline rather than amorphous

(B) the amorphous atomic structure of glass causes it to behave like a very viscous liquid even in its solid form

(C) methods of glass making in medieval times were similar to the methods used in modern times

(D) the transition temperature of the glass used in medieval windows is the same as that of the glass used in modern windows

(E) liquid glass and solid glass are thermodynamically dissimilar

26. Which one of the following is most analogous to the persistent belief about glass described in the passage?

(A) Most people believe that the tendency of certain fabrics to become wrinkled cannot be corrected during the manufacturing process.

(B) Most people believe that certain flaws in early pottery were caused by the material used rather than the process used in manufacturing the pottery.

(C) Most people believe that inadequate knowledge of manufacturing techniques shortens the life span of major appliances.

(D) Most people believe that modern furniture made on an assembly line is inferior to individually crafted furniture.

(E) Most people believe that modern buildings are able to withstand earthquakes because they are made from more durable materials than were older buildings.

27. The passage suggests that which one of the following statements accurately characterizes the transition temperature of glass?

(A) It is higher for medieval glass than for modern glass.

(B) It has only recently been calculated with precision.

(C) Its upper extreme is well above 350 degrees Celsius.

(D) It does not affect the tendency of some kinds of glass to flow downward.

(E) For some types of glass, it is a specific temperature well below 350 degrees Celsius.

S T O P

IF YOU FINISH BEFORE TIME IS CALLED, YOU MAY CHECK YOUR WORK ON THIS SECTION ONLY.
DO NOT WORK ON ANY OTHER SECTION IN THE TEST.

SECTION III
Time—35 minutes
25 Questions

Directions: The questions in this section are based on the reasoning contained in brief statements or passages. For some questions, more than one of the choices could conceivably answer the question. However, you are to choose the best answer; that is, the response that most accurately and completely answers the question. You should not make assumptions that are by commonsense standards implausible, superfluous, or incompatible with the passage. After you have chosen the best answer, blacken the corresponding space on your answer sheet.

1. When industries rapidly apply new technology, people who possess the skills and knowledge to master it prosper, while many others lose their jobs. But firms that resist technological innovations will eventually be superseded by those that do not, resulting in the loss of all their employees' jobs. Obviously, then, resisting the application of new technology in industry _____.

   Which one of the following most logically completes the argument?

   (A) is less likely to dislocate workers than it is to create job security for them
   (B) will affect only those who possess technical skills
   (C) cannot prevent job loss in the long run
   (D) eventually creates more jobs than it destroys
   (E) must take priority over any attempt to promote new industries

2. While sales of other highly fuel-efficient automobiles are in decline, sales of the Hydro are rising. The Hydro's manufacturers attribute its success to the Hydro's price and very low fuel consumption. However, the Hydro is comparable in price and fuel efficiency to its competitors, so it is more likely that its success is due to the fact that people want to appear environmentally conscious to their neighbors.

   Which one of the following is an assumption required by the argument?

   (A) The Hydro is the most popular highly fuel-efficient automobile available.
   (B) The Hydro is recognizable as environmentally friendly in a way that its competitors are not.
   (C) The Hydro has a better safety record than its competitors.
   (D) Hydro buyers are more likely to have neighbors who also drive Hydros.
   (E) Hydro buyers have less interest in environmental causes than buyers of other highly fuel-efficient automobiles.

3. Louise McBride, a homeowner, filed a complaint against a nearby nightclub through the Licensing Bureau, a government agency. Although regulations clearly state that Form 283 is to be used for formal complaints, Bureau staff gave McBride Form 5, which she used with the intention of filing a formal complaint. The nightclub argues that the complaint should be dismissed because the incorrect form was used. But that would be unfair.

   Which one of the following principles, if valid, most helps to justify the judgment that dismissing the complaint would be unfair?

   (A) People who wish to file complaints through the Licensing Bureau should be informed of all relevant regulations.
   (B) Government agencies should make their forms straightforward enough that completing them will not be unduly burdensome for the average person.
   (C) It is unfair for someone's complaint to be dismissed because of an incorrect action on the part of a government agency.
   (D) A government agency should not make its procedures so complex that even the agency's employees cannot understand the procedures.
   (E) It is unfair for a business to be subject to a formal complaint unless the complaint is made in a way that provides the business with an opportunity to defend itself.

4. The size of the spleen is a good indicator of how healthy a bird is: sickly birds generally have significantly smaller spleens than healthy birds. Researchers found that, in general, birds that had been killed by predators had substantially smaller spleens than birds killed accidentally.

   Which one of the following is most strongly supported by the information above?

   (A) Predators are unable to kill healthy birds.
   (B) Most birds with smaller than average spleens are killed by predators.
   (C) Predators can sense whether a bird is sick.
   (D) Sickly birds are more likely than healthy birds to be killed by predators.
   (E) Small spleen size is one of the main causes of sickness in birds.

GO ON TO THE NEXT PAGE.

5. Home ownership is a sign of economic prosperity. This makes it somewhat surprising that across the various regions of Europe and North America, high levels of home ownership correspond with high levels of unemployment.

Which one of the following, if true, helps to resolve the apparent conflict described above?

(A) Home ownership makes it more difficult to move to a place where jobs are more plentiful.

(B) Over the last few decades jobs have been moving from centralized areas to locations that are closer to homeowners.

(C) The correspondence between high levels of home ownership and high levels of unemployment holds across countries with widely different social systems.

(D) People who own homes are more likely than those who rent to form support networks that help them to learn of local jobs.

(E) People are more likely to buy homes when they are feeling economically secure.

6. If newly hatched tobacco hornworms in nature first feed on plants from the nightshade family, they will not eat leaves from any other plants thereafter. However, tobacco hornworms will feed on other sorts of plants if they feed on plants other than nightshades just after hatching. To explain this behavior, scientists hypothesize that when a hornworm's first meal is from a nightshade, its taste receptors become habituated to the chemical indioside D, which is found only in nightshades, and after this habituation nothing without indioside D tastes good.

Which one of the following, if true, adds the most support for the hypothesis?

(A) Tobacco hornworms that first fed on nightshade leaves show no preference for any one variety of nightshade plant over any other.

(B) If taste receptors are removed from tobacco hornworms that first fed on nightshade leaves, those hornworms will subsequently feed on other leaves.

(C) Tobacco hornworm eggs are most commonly laid on nightshade plants.

(D) Indioside D is not the only chemical that occurs only in nightshade plants.

(E) The taste receptors of the tobacco hornworm have physiological reactions to several naturally occurring chemicals.

7. Employee: My boss says that my presentation to our accounting team should have included more detail about profit projections. But people's attention tends to wander when they are presented with too much detail. So, clearly my boss is incorrect.

The reasoning in the employee's argument is flawed because the argument

(A) takes for granted that the boss's assessments of employee presentations are generally not accurate

(B) fails to distinguish between more of something and too much of it

(C) fails to consider that an audience's attention might wander for reasons other than being presented with too much detail

(D) infers a generalization based only on a single case

(E) confuses two distinct meanings of the key term "detail"

8. The local news media have long heralded Clemens as an honest politician. They were proven wrong when Clemens was caught up in a corruption scandal. This demonstrates how the local media show too much deference toward public figures. Even the editor of the local newspaper admitted that her reporters neglected to follow leads that might have exposed the scandal far earlier.

Which one of the following most accurately expresses the overall conclusion drawn in the argument?

(A) Clemens has long been portrayed as an honest politician by the local news media.

(B) The local news media were wrong to herald Clemens as an honest politician.

(C) The local news media show too much deference toward public figures.

(D) Reporters from the local newspaper neglected to follow leads that might have exposed the scandal much earlier.

(E) The local newspaper's treatment of Clemens is indicative of its treatment of public figures in general.

GO ON TO THE NEXT PAGE.

9. We know that if life ever existed on the Moon, there would be signs of life there. But numerous excursions to the Moon have failed to provide us with any sign of life. So there has never been life on the Moon.

The pattern of reasoning in the argument above is most similar to that in which one of the following?

(A) We know that the spy is a traitor. We do not know that the general is a traitor. So the general is not a spy.

(B) If we have any mayonnaise, it would be in the refrigerator. But the refrigerator is almost empty. So it is unlikely that we have mayonnaise.

(C) Hendricks will win the election only if voters are concerned primarily with fighting crime. Hendricks is in favor of tougher criminal penalties. So voters will probably go with Hendricks.

(D) If rodents are responsible for the lost grain from last year's harvest, we would find signs of rodents in the warehouses. And we have found signs of rodents there. So rodents are responsible for the lost grain.

(E) If their army is planning an attack, there would either be troop movements along the border or a transfer of weapons. But intelligence reports show no indication of either. So their army is not planning an attack.

10. Television host: While it's true that the defendant presented a strong alibi and considerable exculpatory evidence and was quickly acquitted by the jury, I still believe that there must be good reason to think that the defendant is not completely innocent in the case. Otherwise, the prosecutor would not have brought charges in the first place.

The reasoning in the television host's argument is flawed in that the argument

(A) takes lack of evidence for a view as grounds for concluding that the view is false

(B) presupposes as evidence the conclusion that it is trying to establish

(C) places undue reliance on the judgments of an authority figure

(D) confuses legal standards for guilt with moral standards for guilt

(E) concludes that a judgment is suspicious merely on the grounds that it was reached quickly

11. Literature professor: Critics charge that the work of C. F. Providence's best-known follower, S. N. Sauk, lacks aesthetic merit because it employs Providence's own uniquely potent system of symbolic motifs in the service of a political ideal that Providence—and, significantly, some of these critics as well—would reject. Granting that Sauk is more imitator than innovator, and that he maintained political views very different from those Providence maintained, it has yet to be shown that these facts make his writings any less subtly or powerfully crafted than those of his more esteemed mentor. So the critics' argument should be rejected.

The literature professor argues that the conclusion drawn by the critics has not really been established, on the grounds that

(A) the claims made in support of this conclusion are inaccurate

(B) Sauk's work has aesthetic merit

(C) these critics are motivated by antipathy toward Sauk's political ideas

(D) the claims made in support of this conclusion have not been shown to be correct

(E) the claims made in support of this conclusion have not been shown to be relevant to it

12. Policy: The factory's safety inspector should not approve a new manufacturing process unless it has been used safely for more than a year at another factory or it will demonstrably increase safety at the factory.

Application: The safety inspector should not approve the proposed new welding process, for it cannot be shown to increase safety at the factory.

Which one of the following, if true, justifies the above application of the policy?

(A) The factory at which the new welding process was first introduced has had several problems associated with the process.

(B) The proposed new welding process has not been used in any other factory.

(C) Some of the manufacturing processes currently in use at the factory are not demonstrably safer than the new welding process.

(D) The safety inspector will not approve any new process that has not been used extensively elsewhere.

(E) The proposed new welding process has been used in only one other factory.

GO ON TO THE NEXT PAGE.

13. University administrator: Graduate students incorrectly claim that teaching assistants should be considered university employees and thus entitled to the usual employee benefits. Granted, teaching assistants teach classes, for which they receive financial compensation. However, the sole purpose of having teaching assistants perform services for the university is to enable them to fund their education. If they were not pursuing degrees here or if they could otherwise fund their education, they would not hold their teaching posts at all.

Which one of the following, if true, most seriously weakens the administrator's argument?

(A) The administrator is cognizant of the extra costs involved in granting employee benefits to teaching assistants.

(B) The university employs adjunct instructors who receive compensation similar to that of its teaching assistants.

(C) The university has proposed that in the interest of economy, 10 percent of the faculty be replaced with teaching assistants.

(D) Most teaching assistants earn stipends that exceed their cost of tuition.

(E) Teaching assistants work as much and as hard as do other university employees.

14. Branson: Most of the air pollution in this country comes from our largest cities. These cities would pollute less if they were less populated. So if many people in these cities were to move to rural areas, air pollution in the country as a whole would be reduced.

Which one of the following demonstrates most effectively by parallel reasoning that Branson's argument is flawed?

(A) Similarly, we could conclude that Monique spends most of her salary on housing. After all, people are bound to spend more on housing if they live in a city where the cost of housing is high, and Monique recently moved to a city where the cost of housing is very high.

(B) Similarly, we could conclude that Karen's family would have more living space if they moved from an apartment to a single-family home. After all, single-family homes are typically larger than apartments.

(C) Similarly, we could conclude that most of Ward's farm is planted with corn. After all, in Ward's county most of the fields that used to be planted with other crops are now planted with corn.

(D) Similarly, we could conclude that Javier could consume fewer calories by eating for breakfast, lunch, and dinner only a portion of what he now eats, and eating the remainder as snacks. After all, breakfast, lunch, and dinner together account for most of the calories Javier consumes.

(E) Similarly, we could conclude that most of this city's air pollution would be eliminated if this city built a public transportation system. After all, public transportation produces much less pollution per passenger, and all automobile trips could be replaced by trips on public transportation.

GO ON TO THE NEXT PAGE.

15. Ninety percent of recent car buyers say safety was an important factor in their purchase. Yet of these car buyers, only half consulted objective sources of vehicle safety information before making their purchase; the others relied on advertisements and promotional materials. Thus, these other buyers were mistaken in saying that safety was important to them.

The argument's conclusion follows logically if which one of the following is assumed?

(A) Someone who claims that safety was an important factor in a buying decision does not necessarily mean that safety was the most important factor.

(B) Advertisements and promotional materials sometimes provide incomplete vehicle safety information.

(C) Recent car buyers do not necessarily tell the truth when asked about the factors that contributed to their vehicle purchases.

(D) Most consumers are aware that advertisements and promotional materials are not objective sources of vehicle safety information.

(E) Anyone to whom safety is an important factor in purchasing a car will consult an objective source of vehicle safety information before buying.

16. Theorist: To be capable of planned locomotion, an organism must be able both to form an internal representation of its environment and to send messages to its muscles to control movements. Such an organism must therefore have a central nervous system. Thus, an organism incapable of planned locomotion does not have a central nervous system.

The theorist's argument is flawed in that it

(A) confuses a necessary condition for an organism's possessing a capacity with a sufficient one

(B) takes for granted that organisms capable of sending messages from their central nervous systems to their muscles are also capable of locomotion

(C) presumes, without providing justification, that planned locomotion is the only biologically useful purpose for an organism's forming an internal representation of its environment

(D) takes for granted that adaptations that serve a biologically useful purpose originally came about for that purpose

(E) presumes, without providing justification, that an internal representation of its environment can be formed by an organism with even a rudimentary nervous system

17. Rocket engines are most effective when exhaust gases escape from their nozzles at the same pressure as the surrounding atmosphere. At low altitudes, where atmospheric pressure is high, this effect is best produced by a short nozzle, but when the rocket passes through the thin upper atmosphere, a long nozzle becomes more effective. Thus, to work most effectively throughout their ascents, all rockets must have both short nozzles and long nozzles on their engines.

Which one of the following is an assumption the argument requires?

(A) Equipping a rocket's engines with both short and long nozzles is not significantly more difficult than equipping them with nozzles of equal lengths.

(B) At some point during their ascents, all rockets will pass through the thin upper atmosphere.

(C) A rocket with only short nozzles on its engines cannot reach high altitudes.

(D) For a rocket to work effectively, its engines' exhaust gases must leave the nozzles at the same pressure as the surrounding atmosphere throughout the rocket's ascent.

(E) For a rocket to work most effectively at both low and high atmospheric pressures, it must have at least one engine that has both a short nozzle and a long nozzle.

GO ON TO THE NEXT PAGE.

18. Consumer advocate: Manufacturers of children's toys often place warnings on their products that overstate the dangers their products pose. Product-warning labels should overstate dangers only if doing so reduces injuries. In fact, however, manufacturers overstate their products' dangers merely for the purpose of protecting themselves from lawsuits brought by parents of injured children. Therefore, manufacturers of children's toys should not overstate the dangers their products pose.

Which one of the following most accurately describes a reasoning flaw in the consumer advocate's argument?

(A) The argument confuses a necessary condition for reducing the number of injuries caused by a product with a sufficient condition.

(B) The argument overlooks the possibility that warnings that do not overstate the dangers that their products pose do not always reduce injuries.

(C) The argument relies on a sample that is unlikely to be representative.

(D) The argument presumes, without providing justification, that if a warning overstates a danger, then the warning will fail to prevent injuries.

(E) The argument relies on the unjustified assumption that an action has an effect only if it was performed in order to bring about that effect.

19. A recent study showed that the immune system blood cells of the study's participants who drank tea but no coffee took half as long to respond to germs as did the blood cells of participants who drank coffee but no tea. Thus, drinking tea boosted the participants' immune system defenses.

Which one of the following is an assumption on which the argument depends?

(A) All of the participants in the study drank either tea or coffee, and none drank both.

(B) Coffee has no health benefits that are as valuable as the boost that tea purportedly gives to the body's immune system.

(C) In the study, drinking coffee did not cause the blood cell response time to double.

(D) Coffee drinkers in general are no more likely to exercise and eat healthily than are tea drinkers.

(E) Coffee and tea do not have in common any chemicals that fight disease in the human body.

20. Engineer: Semiplaning monohulls are a new kind of ship that can attain twice the speed of conventional ships. Due to increased fuel needs, transportation will be much more expensive on semiplaning monohulls than on conventional ships. Similarly, travel on jet airplanes was more expensive than travel on other planes at first, but jet airplanes still attracted enough passengers to be profitable, because they offered greater speed and reliability. Semiplaning monohulls offer the same advantages over traditional ships. Thus they will probably be profitable as well.

Which one of the following most accurately describes the role played in the engineer's argument by the statement that transportation will be much more expensive on semiplaning monohulls than on traditional ships?

(A) It serves as one of two analogies drawn between semiplaning monohulls and jet airplanes, which function together to support the argument's main conclusion.

(B) It draws an analogy between semiplaning monohulls and conventional ships that constitutes an objection to the argument's main conclusion, one that is subsequently rejected by appeal to another analogy.

(C) It draws a distinction between characteristics of semiplaning monohulls and characteristics of conventional ships that independently provides support for the argument's main conclusion.

(D) It constitutes a potential objection to the argument's main conclusion, but is subsequently countered by an analogy drawn between ships and airplanes.

(E) It draws a distinction between characteristics of semiplaning monohulls and characteristics of conventional ships that the argument's main conclusion compares to a distinction between types of airplanes.

GO ON TO THE NEXT PAGE.

21. Maté is a beverage found in much of South America. While it is uncertain where maté was first made, there are more varieties of it found in Paraguay than anywhere else. Also, maté is used more widely there than anywhere else. Therefore, Paraguay is likely the place where maté originated.

Which one of the following, if true, would most strengthen the argument?

(A) It is rare for there to be a great variety of types of a beverage in a place where the beverage has not been in use for a very long time.

(B) Many Paraguayans believe that maté became popular at a time when people from other areas of South America were first migrating to Paraguay.

(C) Many Paraguayans believe that the best maté is found in Paraguay.

(D) There are few places outside of South America where maté is regularly consumed.

(E) Typically, the longer a beverage has been in use in a particular place, the more widely that beverage is used there.

22. From 1996 to 2004, the average family income in a certain country decreased by 10 percent, after adjustments for inflation. Opponents of the political party that ruled during this time claim that this was due to mismanagement of the economy by that party.

Each of the following rejoinders, if true, directly counters the opponents' explanation of the decrease in average family income EXCEPT:

(A) There had been a rise in family income in 1996, after adjustments for inflation.

(B) For noneconomic reasons, fewer families had multiple incomes at the end of the period than at the beginning.

(C) During the period, international events beyond the control of the country's government had a negative effect on family incomes in the country.

(D) Younger wage earners usually earn less than older ones, and the average age of household wage earners fell during most years in the past several decades.

(E) The biggest decreases in family income resulted from policies enacted before the ruling party came to power in 1996.

23. Amateur gardeners who plant based on the phases of the moon tend to get better results than those who do not. This seems surprising since the phases of the moon do not affect how plants grow. An alternative practice often found among amateur gardeners is to plant during the first warm spell of spring, which leads to problems when a frost follows. So, amateur gardeners who use the phases of the moon are less likely to lose plants to a frost.

The argument requires assuming which one of the following?

(A) Using the phases of the moon usually leads amateur gardeners to plant later in the spring than those planting at the first warm spell.

(B) The phases of the moon affect whether a frost follows the first warm spell of spring.

(C) Amateur gardeners who use the phases of the moon tend to plant different types of plants than do other amateur gardeners.

(D) Amateur gardeners cannot improve their results unless they understand why their methods work as they do.

(E) Professional gardeners only rarely plant at the first warm spell of spring.

GO ON TO THE NEXT PAGE.

24. Columnist: On average, about 70 percent of the profit from tourism in developing countries goes to foreign owners of tourist businesses. In general, as a country becomes a more established tourist destination, the proportion of revenues exported in this way increases. However, tourists can counteract this effect by obtaining accommodations and other services directly from local people.

Which one of the following is most strongly supported by the statements made by the columnist?

(A) Tourists in a developing nation should obtain accommodations and other services directly from local people if most of the profits from tourism in that nation go to foreign owners of tourist businesses.

(B) In at least some of the developing countries that are most established as tourist destinations, most of the profits from tourism go to foreign owners of tourist businesses.

(C) In at least some developing countries, tourists obtain most of their accommodations and other services directly from local people.

(D) In general, as a developing country becomes a more established tourist destination, local people become progressively poorer.

(E) Tourists who obtain accommodations and other services directly from local people do not contribute in any way to the profits of foreign owners of tourist businesses.

25. The populations of certain species of amphibians have declined dramatically in recent years, an effect many scientists attribute to industrial pollution. However, most amphibian species' populations vary greatly from year to year because of natural variations in the weather. It is therefore impossible to be sure that the recent decline in those amphibian populations is due to industrial pollution.

The argument depends on assuming which one of the following?

(A) The amphibian species whose population declines have been attributed by many scientists to industrial pollution are not known to be among those species whose populations do not vary greatly as a result of natural variations in the weather.

(B) The variations in amphibian species' populations that result from natural variations in the weather are not always as large as the amphibian population declines that scientists have attributed to industrial pollution.

(C) Either industrial pollution or natural variations in the weather, but not both, caused the amphibian population declines that scientists have attributed to industrial pollution.

(D) If industrial pollution were reduced, the decline in certain amphibian populations would be reversed, and if industrial pollution increases, the decline in certain amphibian populations will be exacerbated.

(E) If industrial pollution is severe, it can create more variations in the weather than would occur naturally.

S T O P

IF YOU FINISH BEFORE TIME IS CALLED, YOU MAY CHECK YOUR WORK ON THIS SECTION ONLY.
DO NOT WORK ON ANY OTHER SECTION IN THE TEST.

SECTION IV

Time—35 minutes

23 Questions

Directions: Each group of questions in this section is based on a set of conditions. In answering some of the questions, it may be useful to draw a rough diagram. Choose the response that most accurately and completely answers each question and blacken the corresponding space on your answer sheet.

Questions 1–6

A corporation's Human Resources department must determine annual bonuses for seven employees—Kimura, Lopez, Meng, and Peterson, who work in the Finance department; and Vaughan, Xavier, and Zane, who work in the Graphics department. Each employee will receive either a $1,000 bonus, a $3,000 bonus, or a $5,000 bonus, in accordance with the following:

    No one in the Graphics department receives a $1,000 bonus.

    Any employee who was rated Highly Effective receives a larger bonus than anyone in his or her department who was not rated Highly Effective.

    Only Lopez, Meng, and Xavier were rated Highly Effective.

1. Which one of the following is an allowable distribution of bonuses to the seven employees?

(A)   [Finance] Kimura: $1,000; Lopez: $5,000; Meng: $5,000; Peterson: $1,000
    [Graphics] Vaughan: $3,000; Xavier: $3,000; Zane: $3,000

(B)   [Finance] Kimura: $1,000; Lopez: $5,000; Meng: $5,000; Peterson: $3,000
    [Graphics] Vaughan: $3,000; Xavier: $5,000; Zane: $1,000

(C)   [Finance] Kimura: $1,000; Lopez: $5,000; Meng: $5,000; Peterson: $3,000
    [Graphics] Vaughan: $3,000; Xavier: $5,000; Zane: $3,000

(D)   [Finance] Kimura: $3,000; Lopez: $5,000; Meng: $3,000; Peterson: $1,000
    [Graphics] Vaughan: $3,000; Xavier: $5,000; Zane: $3,000

(E)   [Finance] Kimura: $3,000; Lopez: $5,000; Meng: $5,000; Peterson: $1,000
    [Graphics] Vaughan: $1,000; Xavier: $5,000; Zane: $3,000

GO ON TO THE NEXT PAGE.

2. If Lopez does not receive the same bonus as Meng, which one of the following could be true?

   (A) Kimura receives a $3,000 bonus.
   (B) Lopez receives a $3,000 bonus.
   (C) Peterson receives a $3,000 bonus.
   (D) Kimura receives the same bonus as Vaughan.
   (E) Peterson receives a larger bonus than Kimura.

3. If only one of the employees receives a $1,000 bonus, which one of the following must be true?

   (A) Meng receives a $5,000 bonus.
   (B) Peterson receives a $3,000 bonus.
   (C) Meng receives a $3,000 bonus.
   (D) The employee who receives a $1,000 bonus is Peterson.
   (E) The employee who receives a $1,000 bonus is Kimura.

4. Which one of the following must be true?

   (A) At least one of the employees receives a $1,000 bonus.
   (B) At least three of the employees receive $3,000 bonuses.
   (C) At most three of the employees receive $3,000 bonuses.
   (D) At least two of the employees receive $5,000 bonuses.
   (E) At most three of the employees receive $5,000 bonuses.

5. If exactly two of the employees receive $5,000 bonuses, which one of the following must be true?

   (A) Lopez receives a $3,000 bonus.
   (B) Meng receives a $3,000 bonus.
   (C) Meng is one of the employees who receives a $5,000 bonus.
   (D) Peterson receives a $1,000 bonus.
   (E) Peterson receives a $3,000 bonus.

6. Any of the following could be true of the seven employees EXCEPT:

   (A) The same number receive $1,000 bonuses as receive $3,000 bonuses.
   (B) More receive $1,000 bonuses than receive $3,000 bonuses.
   (C) The same number receive $1,000 bonuses as receive $5,000 bonuses.
   (D) More receive $1,000 bonuses than receive $5,000 bonuses.
   (E) More receive $3,000 bonuses than receive $5,000 bonuses.

GO ON TO THE NEXT PAGE.

Questions 7–11

A landscaper will plant exactly seven trees today—a hickory, a larch, a maple, an oak, a plum, a sycamore, and a walnut. Each tree must be planted on exactly one of three lots—1, 2, or 3—in conformity with the following requirements:

> The trees planted on one lot are the hickory, the oak, and exactly one other tree.
> The maple is not planted on the same lot as the walnut.
> Either the larch or the walnut, but not both, is planted on lot 1.
> Either the maple or the oak, but not both, is planted on lot 2.
> More trees are planted on lot 3 than on lot 1.

7. Which one of the following could be the list of the trees that the landscaper plants on each of the lots today?

(A)   lot 1: the larch, the maple
       lot 2: the hickory, the oak
       lot 3: the plum, the sycamore, the walnut
(B)   lot 1: the larch, the maple
       lot 2: the hickory, the oak, the walnut
       lot 3: the plum, the sycamore
(C)   lot 1: the maple
       lot 2: the hickory, the larch, the oak
       lot 3: the plum, the sycamore, the walnut
(D)   lot 1: the sycamore, the walnut
       lot 2: the larch, the maple
       lot 3: the hickory, the oak, the plum
(E)   lot 1: the walnut
       lot 2: the plum, the sycamore
       lot 3: the hickory, the maple, the oak

GO ON TO THE NEXT PAGE.

8. If the hickory is planted on lot 2, then which one of the following trees must be planted on lot 3?

   (A) the larch
   (B) the maple
   (C) the plum
   (D) the sycamore
   (E) the walnut

9. Which one of the following is a complete and accurate list of the trees any of which could be planted on lot 1?

   (A) the hickory, the plum, the sycamore, the walnut
   (B) the hickory, the sycamore, the walnut
   (C) the larch, the plum, the sycamore, the walnut
   (D) the larch, the plum, the walnut
   (E) the plum, the sycamore, the walnut

10. If the walnut is planted on lot 3, then which one of the following could be true?

    (A) The sycamore is planted on lot 1.
    (B) The hickory is planted on lot 2.
    (C) The larch is planted on lot 2.
    (D) The plum is planted on lot 3.
    (E) The sycamore is planted on lot 3.

11. Where each of the trees is planted is completely determined if which one of the following trees is planted on lot 2?

    (A) the walnut
    (B) the sycamore
    (C) the plum
    (D) the maple
    (E) the larch

GO ON TO THE NEXT PAGE.

4

Questions 12–18

Seven librarians—Flynn, Gomez, Hill, Kitson, Leung, Moore, and Zahn—are being scheduled for desk duty for one week—Monday through Saturday. The librarians will be on duty exactly one day each. On each day except Saturday, there will be exactly one librarian on duty, with two on duty on Saturday, subject to the following constraints:

Hill must be on desk duty earlier in the week than Leung.
Both Hill and Moore must be on desk duty earlier in the week than Gomez.
Flynn must be on desk duty earlier in the week than both Kitson and Moore.
Kitson must be on desk duty earlier in the week than Zahn.
Unless Leung is on desk duty on Saturday, Leung must be on desk duty earlier in the week than Flynn.

12. Which one of the following is an acceptable schedule for the librarians, listed in order from Monday through Saturday?

(A)   Flynn; Hill; Moore; Kitson; Zahn; Gomez and Leung

(B)   Flynn; Moore; Hill; Leung; Kitson; Gomez and Zahn

(C)   Hill; Kitson; Moore; Flynn; Gomez; Leung and Zahn

(D)   Hill; Leung; Flynn; Moore; Zahn; Gomez and Kitson

(E)   Leung; Flynn; Kitson; Moore; Hill; Gomez and Zahn

GO ON TO THE NEXT PAGE.

13. Which one of the following CANNOT be on desk duty on Tuesday?

   (A) Flynn
   (B) Hill
   (C) Kitson
   (D) Moore
   (E) Zahn

14. If Kitson is on desk duty earlier in the week than Moore, which one of the following CANNOT be true?

   (A) Flynn is on desk duty earlier in the week than Leung.
   (B) Gomez is on desk duty earlier in the week than Kitson.
   (C) Gomez is on desk duty earlier in the week than Zahn.
   (D) Hill is on desk duty earlier in the week than Kitson.
   (E) Zahn is on desk duty earlier in the week than Moore.

15. If Zahn is on desk duty on Thursday, which one of the following must be true?

   (A) Flynn is on desk duty earlier in the week than Leung.
   (B) Hill is on desk duty earlier in the week than Flynn.
   (C) Hill is on desk duty earlier in the week than Moore.
   (D) Hill is on desk duty earlier in the week than Zahn.
   (E) Kitson is on desk duty earlier in the week than Moore.

16. If Moore is on desk duty on Tuesday, which one of the following must be true?

   (A) Hill is on desk duty on Thursday.
   (B) Kitson is on desk duty on Thursday.
   (C) Leung is on desk duty on Saturday.
   (D) Zahn is on desk duty on Friday.
   (E) Zahn is on desk duty on Saturday.

17. If Flynn is on desk duty earlier in the week than Hill, which one of the following must be true?

   (A) Hill is on desk duty earlier in the week than Kitson.
   (B) Hill is on desk duty earlier in the week than Zahn.
   (C) Kitson is on desk duty earlier in the week than Moore.
   (D) Moore is on desk duty earlier in the week than Leung.
   (E) Moore is on desk duty earlier in the week than Zahn.

18. Which one of the following, if substituted for the constraint that Flynn must be on desk duty earlier in the week than both Kitson and Moore, would have the same effect in determining the schedule for the librarians?

   (A) Flynn cannot be on desk duty on Thursday.
   (B) Only Flynn or Hill can be on desk duty on Monday.
   (C) Only Hill and Leung can be on desk duty earlier than Flynn.
   (D) Flynn must be on desk duty earlier in the week than both Gomez and Kitson.
   (E) Flynn must be on desk duty earlier in the week than both Moore and Zahn.

GO ON TO THE NEXT PAGE.

Questions 19–23

Each issue of a business newsletter has five slots, numbered 1 through 5. The policy of the newsletter requires that there are at least three features per issue, with each feature completely occupying one or more of the slots. Each feature can be one of four types—finance, industry, marketing, or technology. Any slot not containing a feature contains a graphic. The newsletter's policy further requires that each issue be structured as follows:

Any feature occupying more than one slot must occupy consecutively numbered slots.

If an issue has any finance or technology feature, then a finance or technology feature must occupy slot 1.

An issue can have at most one industry feature.

19. Which one of the following is an allowable structure for an issue of the newsletter?

(A)   slot 1: a finance feature; slot 2: an industry feature; slot 3: a second industry feature; slot 4: a graphic; slot 5: a graphic

(B)   slot 1: a graphic; slot 2: a technology feature; slot 3: a second technology feature; slot 4: a graphic; slot 5: a third technology feature

(C)   slots 1 and 2: a single industry feature; slots 3 and 4: a single marketing feature; slot 5: a finance feature

(D)   slot 1: a technology feature; slots 2 and 3: a single industry feature; slot 4: a finance feature; slot 5: a graphic

(E)   slot 1: a technology feature; slots 2 and 4: a single marketing feature; slot 3: an industry feature; slot 5: a graphic

GO ON TO THE NEXT PAGE.

20. If an issue of the newsletter has no technology feature and if there is a finance feature that occupies both slots 4 and 5, then which one of the following is required for that issue?

(A) A finance feature occupies slot 1.
(B) A finance feature occupies slot 2 or slot 3 or both.
(C) A marketing feature occupies slot 2.
(D) An industry feature or a marketing feature occupies slot 2.
(E) An industry feature or a marketing feature occupies slot 3.

21. Which one of the following is NOT allowed for an issue of the newsletter?

(A) There is exactly one industry feature, and it occupies slot 1.
(B) There is exactly one finance feature, and it occupies slot 2.
(C) There is exactly one technology feature, and it occupies slot 3.
(D) Each feature except the feature occupying slot 1 is either a finance feature or a marketing feature.
(E) Each feature except the feature occupying slot 5 is either an industry feature or a marketing feature.

22. If, in a particular issue of the newsletter, slot 1 is occupied by the only industry feature in that issue, then which one of the following is required for that issue?

(A) There is an industry feature that occupies slots 1 and 2, and only those slots.
(B) There is an industry feature that occupies slots 1, 2, and 3, and only those slots.
(C) There is a marketing feature that occupies slot 2 or slot 3 or both.
(D) There is a marketing feature that occupies one or more of slots 2, 3, and 4.
(E) There is a marketing feature that occupies slot 3 or slot 5 or both.

23. Any of the following is allowed for an issue of the newsletter EXCEPT:

(A) There is exactly one finance feature and no industry or marketing feature.
(B) There is exactly one industry feature and no finance or marketing feature.
(C) There is exactly one industry feature and no marketing or technology feature.
(D) There is exactly one marketing feature and no finance or technology feature.
(E) There is exactly one marketing feature and no industry or technology feature.

S T O P

IF YOU FINISH BEFORE TIME IS CALLED, YOU MAY CHECK YOUR WORK ON THIS SECTION ONLY.
DO NOT WORK ON ANY OTHER SECTION IN THE TEST.

Acknowledgment is made to the following sources from which material has been adapted for use in this test booklet:

Sissela Bok, *Lying: Moral Choice in Public and Private Life*. ©1978 by Sissela Bok.

Sarah M. R. Cravens, "In Pursuit of Actual Justice" in *Alabama Law Review*. ©2007 by Alabama Law Review.

John Palattella, "Pictures of Us." ©1998 by Lingua Franca.

Jeffrey Reiman, "Justice, Civilization, and the Death Penalty." ©1985 by Princeton University Press.

C. Wu, "Analysis Shatters Cathedral Glass Myth." ©1998 by Science Service.

Wait for the supervisor's instructions before you open the page to the topic.
Please print and sign your name and write the date in the designated spaces below.
Time: 35 Minutes

General Directions

u will have 35 minutes in which to plan and write an essay on the topic inside. Read the topic and the accompanying directions carefully. u will probably find it best to spend a few minutes considering the topic and organizing your thoughts before you begin writing. In your essay, sure to develop your ideas fully, leaving time, if possible, to review what you have written. **Do not write on a topic other than the one ecified. Writing on a topic of your own choice is not acceptable.**

special knowledge is required or expected for this writing exercise. Law schools are interested in the reasoning, clarity, organization, guage usage, and writing mechanics displayed in your essay. How well you write is more important than how much you write.

nfine your essay to the blocked, lined area on the front and back of the separate Writing Sample Response Sheet. Only that area will be roduced for law schools. Be sure that your writing is legible.

Both this topic sheet and your response sheet must be turned in to the testing staff before you leave the room.

Topic Code	Print Your Full Name Here		
135161	Last	First	M.I.

Date	Sign Your Name Here
/ /	

Scratch Paper
Do not write your essay in this space.

LSAT® Writing Sample Topic

Directions: The scenario presented below describes two choices, either one of which can be supported on the basis of the information given. Your essay should consider both choices and argue for one over the other, based on the two specified criteria and the facts provided. There is no "right" or "wrong" choice: a reasonable argument can be made for either.

History professor Talia Cordero has just finished a history book manuscript. Two different companies have offered to publish the manuscript, and Cordero must decide which offer to accept. Using the facts below, write an essay in which you argue for one offer over the other based on the following two criteria:

- Cordero wants to maximize the influence her book's ideas have on the study of history.
- Cordero wants to retain as many rights as possible over future use of the book's content.

Penwright Publishing is a major generalized academic press. The principal history journals frequently review Penwright's new history publications. These reviews often influence historians' decisions about what to read. Penwright has been slow to embrace electronic publishing. Their contract would give them exclusive publishing rights to Cordero's manuscript for 25 years. During that time, neither Cordero nor Penwright could allow more than a few paragraphs of the book to be used in other publications without first obtaining the other's permission.

Woodville Press is an up-and-coming academic press focusing on humanities publications. Woodville will soon market a new series of books as being on important topics in history. Cordero's book would be the first publication in the series. To promote the series, Woodville's website would initially offer both electronic and paper copies of the book at a significant discount. Woodville's contract would give them exclusive publishing rights to Cordero's manuscript for 15 years. Throughout that period, other publications authored by Cordero could each include up to one chapter from the book. Woodville would have sole authority over all other publication decisions concerning the book's content.

WP-W135A

Scratch Paper
Do not write your essay in this space.

Writing Sample Response Sheet

DO NOT WRITE IN THIS SPACE

**Begin your essay in the lined area below.
Continue on the back if you need more space.**

COMPUTING YOUR SCORE

Directions:

1. Use the Answer Key on the next page to check your answers.

2. Use the Scoring Worksheet below to compute your raw score.

3. Use the Score Conversion Chart to convert your raw score into the 120–180 scale.

Scoring Worksheet

1. Enter the number of questions you answered correctly in each section.

	Number Correct
SECTION I.............	_____
SECTION II............	_____
SECTION III...........	_____
SECTION IV............	_____

2. Enter the sum here: _____

   This is your Raw Score.

Conversion Chart
For Converting Raw Score to the 120–180 LSAT Scaled Score
LSAT Form 6LSN117

Reported Score	Raw Score Lowest	Raw Score Highest
180	98	100
179	*	*
178	97	97
177	96	96
176	95	95
175	*	*
174	94	94
173	93	93
172	92	92
171	91	91
170	90	90
169	88	89
168	87	87
167	86	86
166	84	85
165	83	83
164	81	82
163	79	80
162	78	78
161	76	77
160	74	75
159	72	73
158	70	71
157	69	69
156	67	68
155	65	66
154	63	64
153	61	62
152	59	60
151	57	58
150	56	56
149	54	55
148	52	53
147	50	51
146	48	49
145	47	47
144	45	46
143	43	44
142	42	42
141	40	41
140	38	39
139	37	37
138	35	36
137	34	34
136	33	33
135	31	32
134	30	30
133	29	29
132	27	28
131	26	26
130	25	25
129	24	24
128	23	23
127	22	22
126	21	21
125	20	20
124	19	19
123	18	18
122	*	*
121	17	17
120	0	16

*There is no raw score that will produce this scaled score for this form.

ANSWER KEY

SECTION I

1.	B	8.	C	15.	C	22.	C
2.	C	9.	A	16.	C	23.	C
3.	A	10.	E	17.	D	24.	E
4.	E	11.	D	18.	B	25.	A
5.	C	12.	D	19.	B		
6.	D	13.	C	20.	E		
7.	E	14.	A	21.	B		

SECTION II

1.	C	8.	B	15.	C	22.	B
2.	A	9.	A	16.	A	23.	A
3.	B	10.	A	17.	D	24.	D
4.	C	11.	C	18.	C	25.	B
5.	A	12.	B	19.	E	26.	B
6.	D	13.	C	20.	B	27.	C
7.	E	14.	E	21.	E		

SECTION III

1.	C	8.	C	15.	E	22.	A
2.	B	9.	E	16.	A	23.	A
3.	C	10.	C	17.	B	24.	B
4.	D	11.	E	18.	E	25.	A
5.	A	12.	B	19.	C		
6.	B	13.	C	20.	D		
7.	B	14.	D	21.	E		

SECTION IV

1.	C	8.	B	15.	A	22.	D
2.	B	9.	C	16.	C	23.	D
3.	A	10.	A	17.	D		
4.	E	11.	A	18.	C		
5.	D	12.	A	19.	D		
6.	B	13.	E	20.	A		
7.	D	14.	B	21.	E		

LSAT® PREP TOOLS

NEW
The Official LSAT SuperPrep II™

SuperPrep II is a brand new book that contains everything you need to prepare for the LSAT—a guide to all three LSAT question types, three actual LSATs, explanations for all questions in the three practice tests, answer keys, writing samples, and score-conversion tables, plus invaluable test-taking instructions to help with pacing and timing. SuperPrep has long been our most comprehensive LSAT preparation book, and SuperPrep II is even better. The practice tests in SuperPrep II are PrepTest 62 (December 2010 LSAT), PrepTest 63 (June 2011 LSAT), and one test that has never before been disclosed.

With this book you can

- Practice on genuine LSAT questions
- Review explanations for right and wrong answers
- Target specific categories for intensive review
- Simulate actual LSAT conditions

LSAC sets the standard for LSAT prep—and SuperPrep II raises the bar!

$32 at LSAC.org

LSAC.org